Embroidery
BASICS

Happy Stitching!
Cheryl Fall

0 11557 01093 0

Embroidery
BASICS

A NeedleKnowledge® Book

Cheryl Fall

STACKPOLE
BOOKS

This book is dedicated to two very important men in my life—My dad, Nelson, who learned to embroider from his grandmother and wasn't afraid to pick up a needle and stitch, and my patient and supportive hubby of thirty years, Tony. Both of these remarkable men understand the relaxation value of stitching and never seem to mind when the ladies of the family are lost in their needlework.

Copyright ©2013 by Stackpole Books

Published by
STACKPOLE BOOKS
5067 Ritter Road
Mechanicsburg, PA 17055
www.stackpolebooks.com

Note: Every effort has been made to ensure the accuracy and completeness of the material presented in this book. The publisher and the author disclaim responsibility for errors, variations in an individual's work, or the use of materials other than those specified.

Printed in the United States of America

10 9 8 7 6 5 4 3 2 1

FIRST EDITION

Cover design by Caroline Stover

Library of Congress Cataloging-in-Publication Data

Fall, Cheryl.
    Embroidery Basics : A NeedleKnowledge Book / Cheryl Fall. -- FIRST EDITION.
        pages   cm
    Includes index.
    ISBN 978-0-8117-1093-0 (pbk.)
    1. Embroidery. I. Title.
TT770.F35   2013
746.44--dc23
                                                    2012021213

Contents

Preface   vi

Supplies and Tools   1

Essential Techniques   13

Embroidery Stitches   17

Embroidery Projects   47

Surface Embroidery Projects

    Tutti-Frutti Three-Piece Kitchen Towel Set   48

    Martini Cocktail Napkins   51

    Embroidered Bag with Shisha Mirrors   53

    Summer Lavender Two-Piece Pillowcase Set   66

    Chain Stitch Blossoms Pillow Top   58

    Alphabet Sampler in Surface Stitches
        with Matching Needle Case   61

    Freestyle Embroidered Purse   66

    Monogram with Padded Satin Stitch   68

    Owl Pincushion   71

    Owl Tablet Cover   74

    Happy Halloween Framed Redwork   76

Counted-Thread Embroidery Projects

    Italian Cross-Stitch Sampler
        with Pin Roll and Scissor Fob   79

    Assisi-Style Tissue Holder   85

    Drawn Thread Square Doily   89

    Flower Basket Journal   92

    Cross-Stitch Snowflake Ornaments   95

    Blackwork Mini-Sampler   97

Finishing Touches   99

Color Conversion and Metric Equivalent Charts   103

Glossary   104

Sources   105

Index of Stitches   106

Preface

I've been stitching embroidery projects since I was a little girl. My first work basket consisted of a metal cookie tin filled with odds and ends my mother gave me. The tin contained a small set of unfinished doilies from the 1950s with pink roses. I loved the design, and at the age of six had the entire set completed. From that moment on, I was hooked.

One of the things I love best about embroidery is its versatility. If I don't like the colors used in a project, I can change them to suit my vision of the finished item. Embroidery can be worked on yardage or stitched onto myriad useful or decorative ready-made items, saving time while I create unique pieces of embroidered art.

Designs for embroidery can range from simple, singular designs to highly elaborate patterns in a single color or multiple colors. The choice is yours, and the possibilities are endless.

This book, filled with full-color photos and illustrations, begins with basic *needle knowledge* and shows you how to use a variety of embroidery threads and simple stitches to create beautiful embroidered projects for the home or to give as gifts. You'll learn the basics and explore hand embroidery from beginner through intermediate levels using the stitches and projects in this book.

A hearty thank-you goes out to my friends at DMC Threads in Kearny, New Jersey. In addition to supplying the bulk of the materials used in this book, they've also been a source of inspiration, great ideas, and a good laugh when things got rough.

If am grateful to my grown daughters, Rebecca and Ashley, whose fresh, youthful ideas always inspire me to push the limits with my designs and to "think young."

To Mary Nevius, I'd like to express my gratitude for her years of friendship and her hard work on the NeedleKnowledge® website.

I'd also like to thank my editor, Kyle Weaver, for asking me to write this book, and the entire Stackpole Books staff, for their work on its publication. It's been a pleasure working with all of you, and I look forward to the next project.

Supplies and Tools

The popularity of embroidery has been soaring over the past few years and with good reason. Embroidery is easy, fun, and doesn't require you to schlep around a huge amount of tools or supplies, making this form of needlework portable and easy to tuck into your handbag.

To create an embroidered project, you'll need some basic supplies, which can be found in most hobby store chains as well as specialty needlework shops.

Here you'll find information on the various threads and fibers, fabrics, and tools needed for embroidery, as well as recommendations on a few items that may not be necessary, but are nice to have on hand.

Threads and Fibers

Thread is to the embroiderer what paint is to the artist. It's the medium that turns a blank fabric into a work of art. There are many different types and sizes of threads available for embroidery, from soft cottons with a matte or glossy finish to wooly textured threads and metallic fibers or holographic threads that dazzle. Threads can be a single color or combine several complementary or contrasting colors twisted in the fibers, or along the length of the thread using dyed effects. The type of thread chosen depends entirely on the look you want to achieve, and the possibilities are endless! Here are some of the popular choices for hand embroidery.

Embroidery Floss

Often referred to as *six-strand floss*, or just shortened to *floss*, this is a mercerized cotton thread consisting of six individual strands. These strands can be separated and used singly or in groups, depending on the desired thickness of the finished embroidery design. Floss is available in a wide range of colors. For example, the DMC Color Card features 454 solid, 18 variegated, and 36 multicolored varieties.

Embroidery floss is available on a pull skein. You simply pull the end of the thread to length and cut. When using floss, lengths should be no longer than the length of your arm, or about 18 inches. Longer lengths are harder to stitch, can cause wear on the thread from the repeated in-and-out motion of stitching, and can tangle easier than shorter lengths.

TIP: Completely separate all strands of embroidery floss and regroup them before using them. This will result in a smoother finished stitch and help prevent tangling.

Pearl Cotton

Pearl cotton is available in skeins or rolled on balls and is available in a variety of weights, from very fine to thick and chunky. The size of pearl cotton you choose depends on the look you want to achieve.

Finer pearl cotton weights, such as sizes 80 through 20, are ideal while using drawn thread techniques and midweight varieties, such as size 12 through 5, are better suited to surface embroidery and cross-stitch or counted-thread projects. The thickest pearl cotton is size 3, which works best on chunky, rustic projects worked in surface embroidery, or in counted-thread techniques on coarse or loosely woven fabrics, such as 7- to 10-count evenweave or 6- to 11-count Aida fabric.

When purchasing pearl cotton (or any other thread), remember that the higher the number, the finer the thread. For example, size 12 pearl cotton thread is going to be much thinner than a size 3 pearl cotton thread.

Wool, Silk, Bamboo, and Linen Threads

A variety of natural fibers are available in both floss and pearl types as well as single-strand yarn, and include threads made from fine wools, silk and silk blends, linen,

Thread Conditioners and Beeswax

Threads such as rayon, satin, and Mylar can be unruly to work with and may snag or tangle back on themselves as you stitch. Using a thread conditioner, like Thread Heaven, or beeswax can help tame the beast. Conditioners and beeswax lubricate the thread, making it easier to pull through the fabric, and also help keep the fibers in the thread together in a tidy bundle.

To use thread conditioner or beeswax, simply run your working thread along the surface of the conditioner after threading your needle and stitch normally. Do not apply too much or your thread could end up gummy or sticky. A fine, invisible layer is all you need, and the conditioner should not be noticeable on the surface of the thread.

and bamboo. Wool varieties are most commonly available as a floss, tapestry, or Persian yarn for crewel and needle-point projects. Bamboo and linen are available in floss, and silk is available in either a floss or pearl variety. These threads can be expensive, but are a joy to stitch with.

Novelty, Metallic, and Holographic Threads

Put some razzle in your dazzle! Use novelty, metallic, or holographic embroidery threads to add a sparkling element to your creations. These threads come in a variety of materials and weights, including multicolored, twisted fibers in narrow or chunky weights, a single narrow filament, or flat ribbon.

Novelty threads can be used to add unique effects to a project, including glow-in-the-dark properties, a pearlized luster, or a dazzling sheen to the stitching in a design. These threads can be used alone in a project or combined with other threads in your needle as a blending filament.

Metallic threads are available in floss and pearl cotton types, as well as single-strand varieties in gold, silver, bronze, copper, and antique metallic varieties. Holographic threads can be a single color or feature a rainbow of colors in a single thread and are available in bright colors as well as metallic styles.

Wired Threads

Fiber-wrapped wire threads can be used to add dimension and texture to an embroidery project. Two popular wired threads are DMC's Color Infusions Memory Thread and Kreinik's HotWire Thread.

Wired threads are not embroidery threads per se. These threads are not worked through the fabric, but instead are secured to the top of the fabric by couching them into place. These threads add an extra layer of dimension to an embroidery project when used to outline key components of a design.

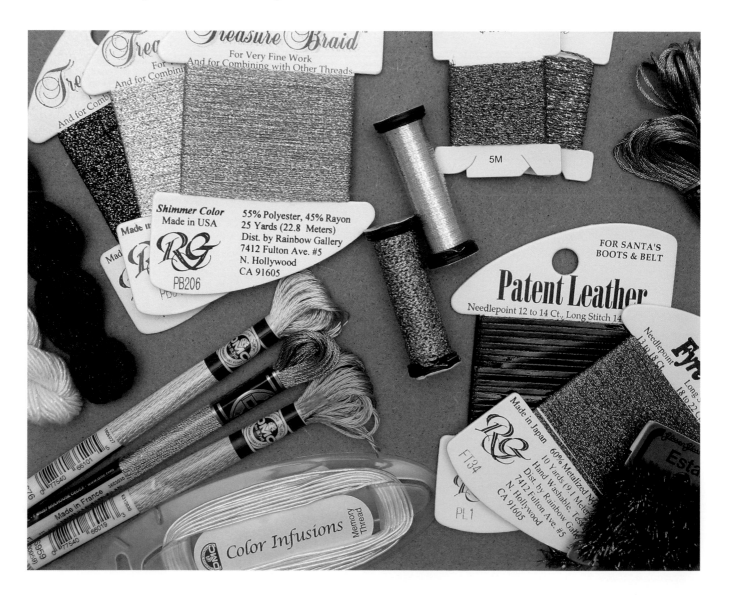

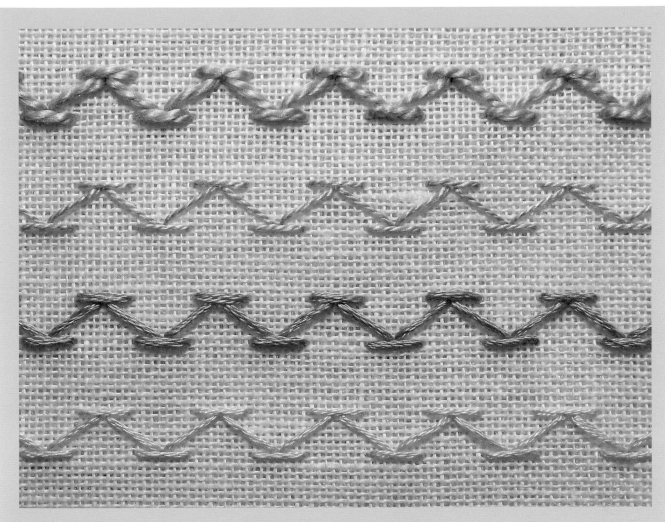

Determining Stitch Gauge

While I'm designing a project, I often stitch a sample to test the gauge to make sure the thread I have chosen is best suited to the design or type of project. In this example, I have worked the same stitch over the same number of threads in an evenweave fabric. As you can see, the look is very different, depending on the thread chosen.

If you are substituting a thread from your collection with the materials called for in a project, I recommend working a gauge sample to be certain the thread will give the proper look or texture to your project before stitching. It's much easier to test first than to rip out stitches and rework the design later.

Fabrics for Embroidery

Embroidery can be worked on virtually any fabric. As long as you can get a needle through it, it's fair game. There are, however, fabrics that are common to embroidery and available at nearly any sewing or embroidery retailer.

Fabrics that have an equal number of warp (vertical) and weft (horizontal) threads that can be easily counted are called *evenweave* fabrics. These fabrics can be very loose or tightly woven. Cotton, linen, cotton/linen blends, bamboo, and wool fabrics are the most common types of evenweave used for embroidery.

The loosely woven varieties such as 28-count linen are perfect for using with counted-thread techniques, including cross-stitch, counted-thread surface embroidery, pulled thread, and drawn-thread projects, because it is easy to count the number of threads in the fabric, aiding in stitch placement. Stitches are worked over a specific number of threads designated in the pattern or project instructions. For example, cross-stitch on evenweave fabric is worked over two threads.

Fabric that is tightly woven and has warp and weft threads that are too tight to count with the naked eye are referred to as *plainweave* fabrics. Plainweave fabrics can

Plain-weave fabrics are suitable for surface embroidery and fine counted work.

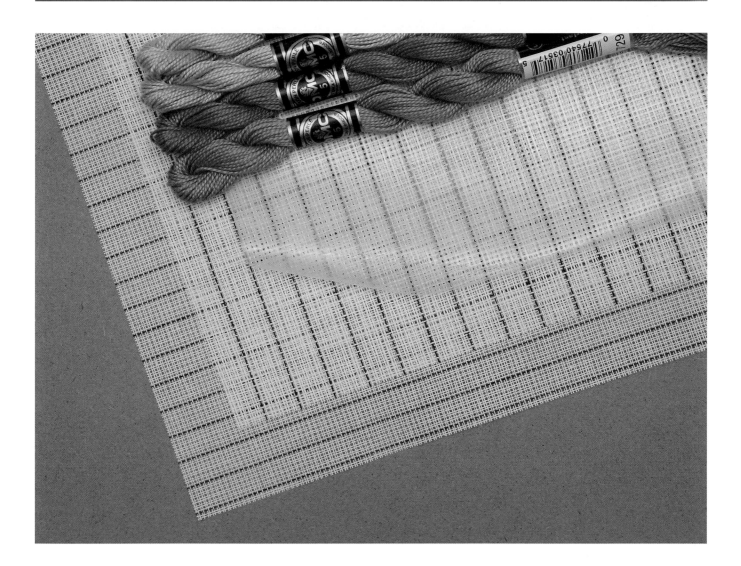

be made from any fiber, but cotton, linen, wool, and poly-ester/cotton blends are most common. Plainweave fabrics can be solid or printed and are used for surface embroidery projects.

TIP: After working, a perfectly square design often ends up oblong rather having four equal sides. This is due to stitch tension; it can be corrected by blocking the finished piece.

Aida is an embroidery fabric that is considered an even-weave, because of the special way the fabric is woven. Clusters of threads in the warp and weft create a fabric grid. This grid is perfect for working a cross-stitch design.

A wide variety of counts are available in Aida fabric, from a very fine 22 squares per inch to a chunky 8 squares. Remember, the smaller the fabric count, the larger the finished project will be.

If you want to embroider a counted design on a plain-weave or heavyweight fabric, stitch the design using *waste canvas* as a guide. There are two types of waste canvas

available: waste canvas and water-soluble waste canvas. Both are temporary and are removed from the fabric ground after stitching by drawing out the threads of the canvas or dissolving the canvas in soapy water.

Estimating Fabric Sizes

If you are unable to locate a particular fabric, or want to make a change to the size of a design, it's easy to estimate the amount of fabric needed for a counted-thread or cross-stitch project. All you need are the pattern and a calculator.

We'll use a cross-stitch pattern as an example. First, count the number of vertical and horizontal stitches in a design. Let's say a pattern is made up of 24 vertical and 24 horizontal stitches.

Now do the math: If the pattern is being worked on 12-count fabric, the design would measure 2 inches square, because 24 stitches divided by 12 squares in the fabric equals 2 inches.

Now, let's figure out the measurement of the design worked on 16-count fabric. That is 24 stitches divided by

16 squares, which equals 1.5. This means the finished size of the design shrinks to 1½ inches square.

But there's more to selecting fabric size than just the count. You'll also need a wide border around the fabric, so that you have a place to hold onto while working the design. I like to estimate an additional 5 to 10 inches around all four sides of a project to give me plenty of room to work. Often, the excess is cut away later and depends entirely on how the project will be finished. The fabric sizes given in this book take these factors into consideration when recommending fabric sizes.

Embroidery on Ready-Made and Unusual Items

A wide variety of ready-made items are available for embroidery, including kitchen and guest towels with Aida bands, bibs and baby items, afghans, and more. But don't limit yourself to items made specifically for embroidery.

Nearly any fabric surface can be enhanced with embroidery. Purses and bags, clothing, sheets and cushion covers, placemats, napkins, and tablecloths are all perfect backdrops for embroidery.

Examples of embroidery on ready-made items can be found in the Summer Lavender Pillowcase Set (page 56) and the Freestyle Embroidered Purse (page 66). These projects use items that were previously made and have been embellished with a variety of embroidery stitches.

Paper can also be used for embroidery. Counted stitches like cross-stitch can be worked on paper canvas, and surface embroidery can be worked on card stock to create one-of-a-kind note cards and tags.

Needle Selection

The needle chosen for a project depends on the weight of the thread you are using and the fabric you are stitching on. Needles for embroidery range from fine, sharp needles with small eyes to chunky needles with long eyes and rounded tips. Each project in this book is accompanied by a needle recommendation.

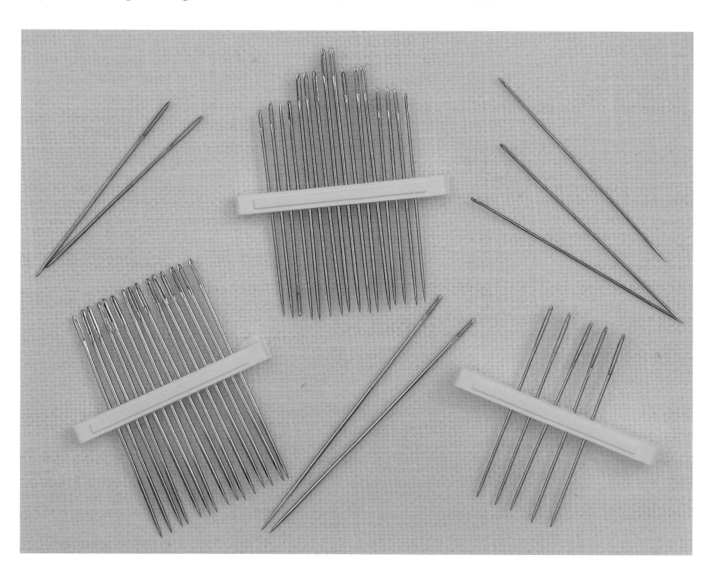

Sharps and *milliners needles* with small eyes are used on projects with fine threads. *Crewel needles* have sharp points and larger eyes and can be used on evenweave and plainweave fabrics with a wide range of thread thicknesses. As the needle size increases, so does the size of the eye and length of the needle, making it easier to pass thicker threads through the eye. These needles are used when the needle needs to *pierce* the fabric when creating a stitch.

Blunt needles, called *ball point needles*, include tapestry and cross-stitch needles and are used on fabrics where the needle needs to slip *between* the threads. Counted cross-stitch on Aida or evenweave fabrics are examples where the needle slips between the threads in the fabric, creating a well-formed stitch.

Notions

Tools for working embroidery projects are minimal and inexpensive. You'll need the following for nearly any embroidery project:

- fabric and thread
- embroidery pattern
- assorted needles (purchasing packets of multiple-sized needles will give you a range to choose from)
- straight pins, for assembly and holding things in place
- scissors and snips
- thimbles in metal, rubber, or leather
- tweezers, for removing small bits of thread (the ones with a magnifying glass are particularly useful)
- embroidery hoops in 6-, 8-, and 12-inch diameters
- ruler or retractable tape measure
- water-soluble marking pens and pencils (not to be confused with transfer pens and pencils, which are *permanent*), for temporarily marking patterns and placement

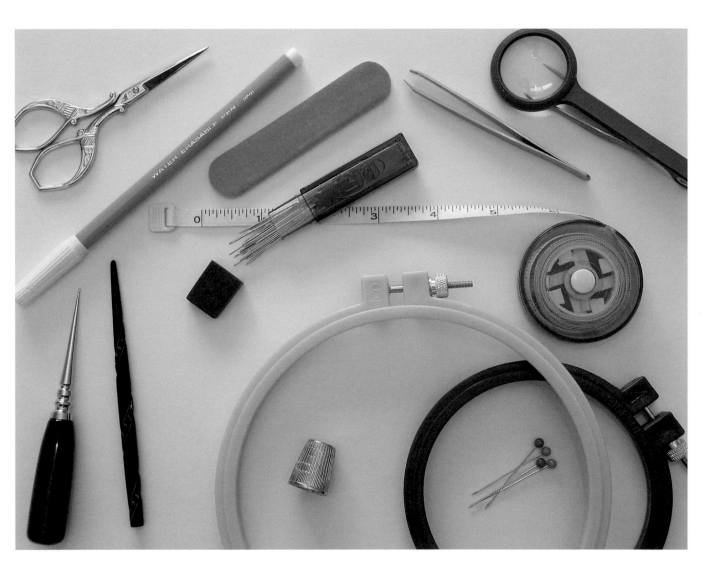

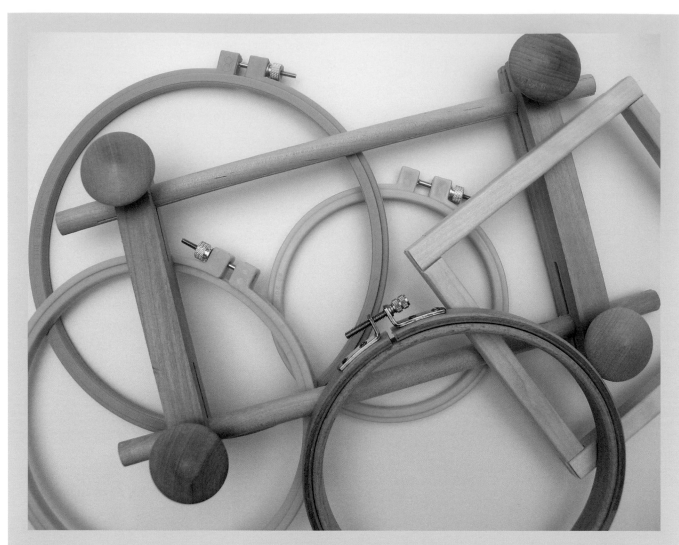

Using an Embroidery Hoop

An embroidery hoop is a double ring of plastic or wood that is used to keep the fabric taut as you work the stitching in a project. Hoops are available in a wide range of sizes from 3 inches on up to 12 inches and larger.

To use an embroidery hoop, transfer the embroidery design to the fabric and select a hoop that is slightly larger than the area you wish to work on. On larger projects, the hoop can be smaller and moved from one section to another as you work.

Loosen the screw or nut on the outer ring and remove the inner ring. Center the embroidery fabric over the inner ring and place the outer ring over the fabric and inner ring. Tighten the screw or nut securely while tugging the fabric from all sides to make it tight in the hoop.

Embroidery hoops should always be removed from the fabric when you put your project away for the day, as the hoop can cause creases that can become permanent if left in place too long.

- good lighting, for selecting colors and to avoid eye strain while stitching (natural light is best, but full-spectrum lighting—available at hobby and sewing stores—that simulates natural light is available and worth purchasing)

Here are some other notions that are not necessary, but are helpful to have on hand:

- stitch gauges, to help you determine fabric thread counts

- magnetic needle cases, to keep your pins and needles safe

- plastic or paper thread bobbins, for storing unwound floss or lengths of unused thread

- laying tools or awls, for keeping threads smooth or making eyelets

- pincushions (you can make your own, like the owl on page 71)

- magnetic pattern holders, to keep your pattern upright and within sight as you stitch

- nail file, just in case you have a burr that catches your thread

Using a Laying Tool

A laying tool is a tool with a tapering shaft, similar to an awl, that is used to help *lay* the threads in a project. Using this tool ensures that your threads lie flat and are not twisted or overlapping each other when working satin stitch or other stitches that are worked closely together.

To use a laying tool, work a stitch, having the tool under the thread. As the thread is pulled towards the fabric, pull the laying tool away while leaving the thread against the tool, guiding the thread into position. You can shimmy the tool a bit as you pull to keep the threads flat against the shaft.

Keeping it All Together

Your supplies can be kept in nearly any type of container including a basket, tote, cookie tin, or box. It's really just a matter of preference. Special bags and holders for needlework are available at craft and needlework stores and are made to hold floss and threads without tangling.

Because I always have multiple projects in the works at the same time, I like to keep my materials in stacking wicker tray-type baskets that are easily accessible. But, when I'm on the go, I prefer a heavy-duty zippered plastic tote bag.

Regardless of what you keep the materials in, do keep your scissors, needles, and other sharp or small objects safely contained in a small, clear zippered pouch. You'll always know where to find your items without the risk of being jabbed while digging through your supplies.

Essential Techniques

The Knot-Free Zone

When working an embroidery pattern, it's always better not to have any knots in the project. While this might seem like an impossible task, it's actually very easy to accomplish.

There are two basic types of knots used to start a length of thread, the *away knot* and the *waste knot*. Both of these start with a knot at the end of the thread, but the knot is removed after working the stitching.

Away knot. For surface embroidery, an away knot works best. To work an away knot, thread your needle and knot the far end of your thread. Insert the needle through the fabric about 6 inches from the point where you will begin embroidering. Work several stitches and then clip the knot. Thread the resulting tail through a needle and weave the tail through the stitching on the back side of the work.

Waste knot. For cross-stitch, a waste knot works best. To work a waste knot, thread your needle and make a knot at the far end of the thread. Insert the needle into the fabric a few stitches in from where the stitching will begin. Stitch over the tail of the thread to secure it and trim away the knot.

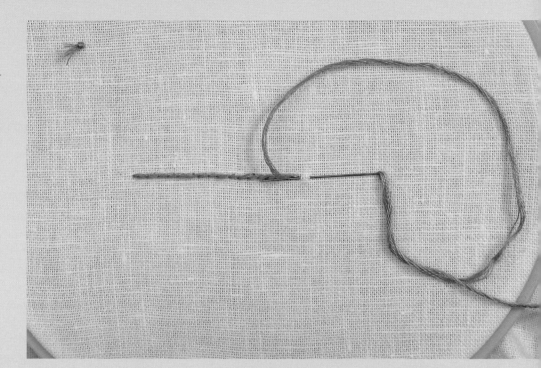

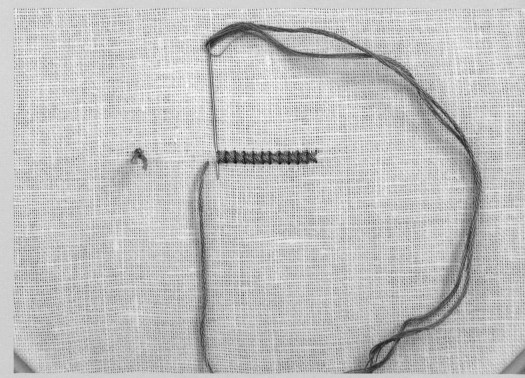

Finishing the thread. Weave the tail through the back side of the stitching on the wrong side of the fabric and cut away the excess. Always run your needle under the stitching to keep the thread as flat as possible, not over it in a whipping motion, as this can add bulk to the back of the fabric.

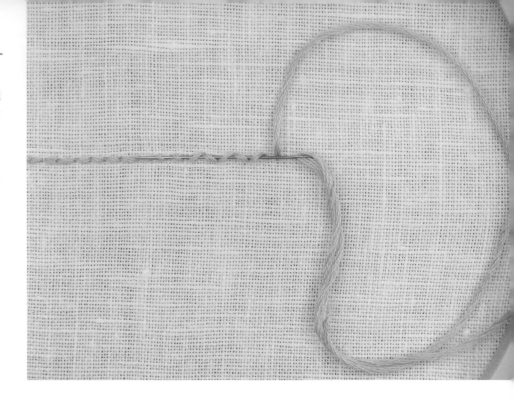

Using a Hank of Embroidery Thread or Pearl Cotton

Hanks of embroidery floss and pearl cotton are wrapped and packaged in a way that makes it easy for the stitcher to pull and cut lengths of thread that are the proper length for stitching. It's really very foolproof if you follow these easy tips.

Embroidery floss is available in a pull skein put-up. This means that the thread is pulled from the skein to the desired length. To do this, find the end of the floss, usually located near the paper band that contains the color number. Pull the thread until you have a 14- to 16-inch length of thread and cut the thread. Separate the thread into the necessary number of strands and thread your needle.

Pearl cotton is woven in a hank and cannot be pulled. If you pull, you'll end up with a knotted mess of thread. These hanks are easy to prepare so that you have perfectly cut length that won't tangle. To prepare a hank, look at the ends. One end has a single loop of twisted thread and the

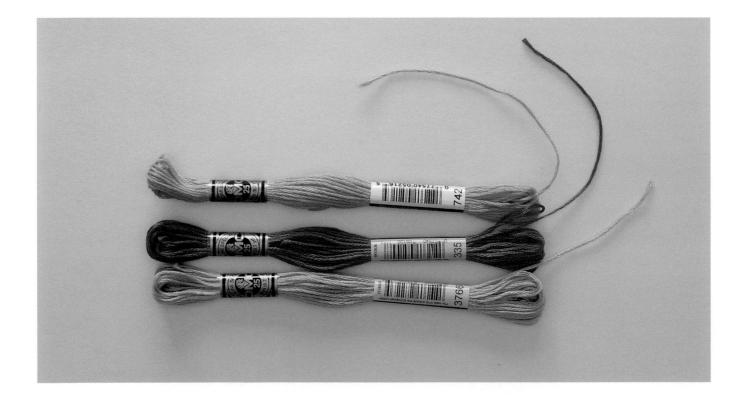

opposite end (usually the end with the band featuring the color number) has two smaller loops of twisted thread.

Using your scissors, cut the two smaller loops of thread. Pull the individual threads from the hank from the uncut end. You'll find that you have perfectly sized 16-inch lengths of thread, ready to use and held neatly together by the paper bands.

Edge-Finishing Techniques

The raw edges of any embroidery fabric should be secured before working any of the stitching. This will help avoid the fabric unraveling as you work. There are several different methods you can use to edge-finish your fabrics:

- hemming
- overstitching with zigzag stitches
- seam sealant
- pinking shears

I like to make all of the needed hems on napkins, tablecloths, sheets, and garments (or anything else that will be hemmed) before working the embroidery. The edges are then pre-finished and it's one less thing I have to do later.

Items that will be finished as pillows and framed art can be edge-finished with overcasting using the zigzag feature of your sewing machine or using a single-turned hem. For items that will be cut from the fabric after working the embroidery, the fabrics can be temporarily finished with seam sealant by running a small bead of sealant along the raw edges or by cutting along the edges of the fabric using pinking shears, creating a zigzagging, sawtooth-cut edge that resists fraying.

Nonwoven fabrics like felt or felted wool do not require edge finishing and can be cut or pinked without fraying.

How to Read a Pattern

The patterns in this book are either line drawings for surface embroidery or charted drawings for counted-thread embroidery. Both types are very easy to follow.

To follow a pattern for a surface-embroidered design, refer to the stitch key for color placement and the stitch uses for each part of the pattern.

Patterns for charted designs indicate one stitch for every square on the fabric.

Transferring a Design to Fabric

Designs for surface embroidery can be transferred to the surface of the fabric using several different transfer methods.

The easiest method is to trace the design directly onto the fabric using a water-soluble fabric marking pen or pencil. To do this, place the pattern over a light source, such as a window or light box, and center the fabric over the

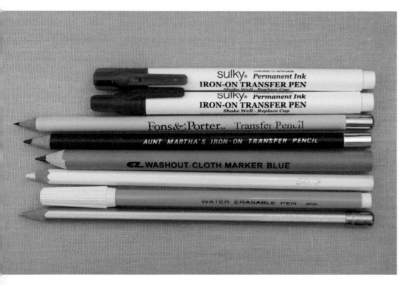

pattern. You should be able to see the design through the fabric and trace it.

You can also use transfer paper made for fabric, which you can find at any sewing or fabric store, to mark the design on the fabric. Place the fabric on a hard surface and place a sheet of transfer paper ink-side-down on the fabric. (The transfer ink side of the paper often has a powdery or waxy feeling to it if you have difficulty determining which side the ink is on.) Center the pattern over the transfer paper and trace the design using a ballpoint pen or stylus.

Tracing designs to heavy fabrics can be done with a technique called *thread tracing*. To transfer using this method, trace the pattern onto a lightweight piece of tracing paper or pattern tissue. Thread a needle with a length of fine thread in a contrasting color. Stitching through both the paper and the fabric, work the running stitch or back stitch along all the marked lines in the pattern. Remove the paper and the thread lines remain on the fabric. Work the final stitching over these fine-stitched lines.

Working with Iron-On Transfers

Heat transfer pens and pencils or ready-made hot-iron transfer patterns can also be used for marking an embroidery pattern. Keep in mind that these markings are permanent and must be completely covered by the embroidery stitches or they will always show on the finished project.

When transferring a design to fabric using this method, remember that you will be creating a mirror image of the design. This means that the design needs to be traced onto the paper using the transfer pen or pencil in *reverse*. While this may not be much of a problem with repeating designs, it's critical for one-way designs and text.

Following the manufacturer's directions and using the proper pressing techniques when transferring a design with this method is essential. Your goal is to have a fine, smooth line to stitch along instead of a smeared line that is difficult to cover.

To press the design onto the fabric properly, never use a side-to-side motion when moving the iron from one area to another. This causes the ink to smear. Instead, carefully lift the iron, move it to the next location, and press downwards.

Embroidery Stitches

Now that you've gathered your supplies and reviewed the basics, it's time to stitch. Refer to the following stitch diagrams to work the projects in this book. A handy index of the stitches, listed in alphabetical order, can be found on page 106 for your reference.

Not all of these stitches have been used in the projects, but they have been included so that you can make stitch substitutions when inspiration happens—and it does happen. You may wish to use a thicker, thinner, or more decorative stitch than the one recommended in the project. Make it your own, get creative, and start stitching!

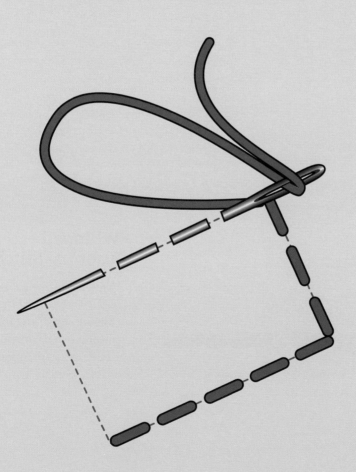

Running Stitch

Running stitch is the stitch that nearly all those who have held needles in their hands learn first. The running stitch is worked using a basic, almost intuitive in-and-out motion of the needle. This stitch is typically used to outline a shape. It can be worked in any length, but should be kept consistent throughout the area being stitched. Running stitch is also functional and can be used to sew pieces of a project together or for basting.

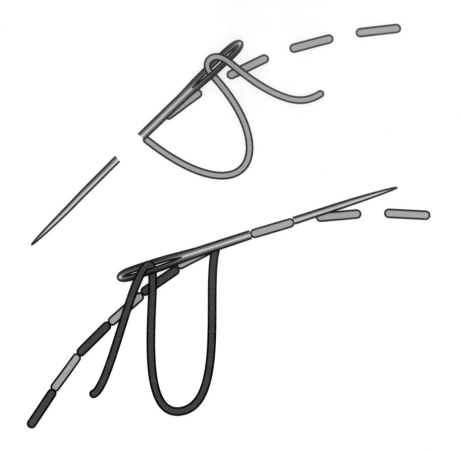

Double Running Stitch

Double running stitch is a decorative stitch worked in two passes of regular running stitch, creating a solid line of stitching. It can be worked in a single color or in two colors.

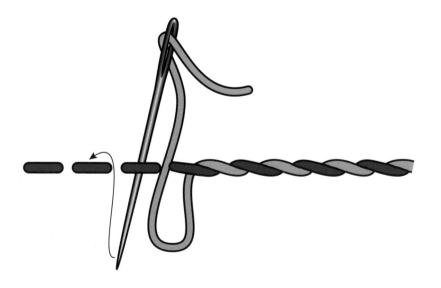

Whipped Running Stitch

Whipped running stitch is worked in two passes. The first pass is the basic running stitch, and the second pass is worked in a whipping motion using a different color, creating a ropelike effect.

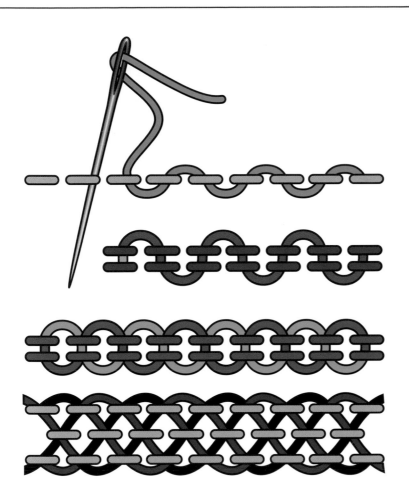

Laced Running Stitch

Laced running stitch is worked through evenly spaced rows of running stitch, with a second color of thread passing in and out of the stitches like a shoelace. Work the lacing through several rows of running stitch for a thicker border or through just two rows for a thinner line of stitching. There's no limit to the number of rows of possibilities when using this stitch; several variations are shown here.

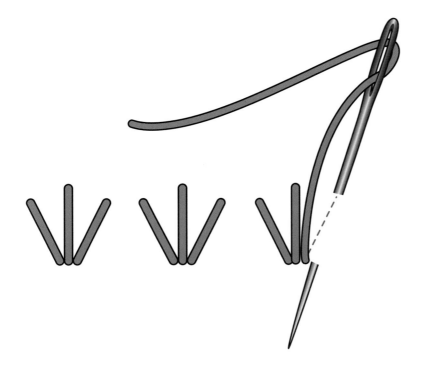

Straight Stitch

Straight stitch is just a single stitch, but can be used in different lengths and in groups to make other stitches or motifs. In this example, three running stitches have been used to make a decorative, repeating element in a border.

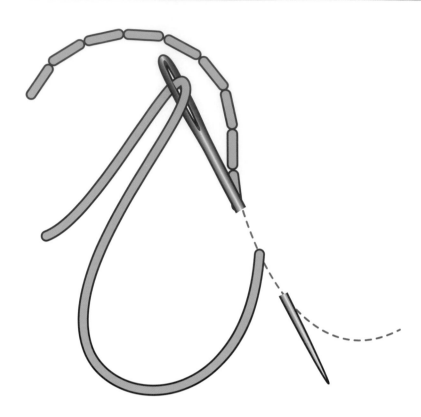

Back Stitch

Back stitch is used to outline a shape and is worked in a motion of two steps forward and one step back. To work the stitch, bring the needle up through the fabric a stitch length's distance from the starting point and insert the needle at the starting point, working the stitch backwards. Bring the needle up again a stitch length's distance from the first stitch and continue working in this manner to the end.

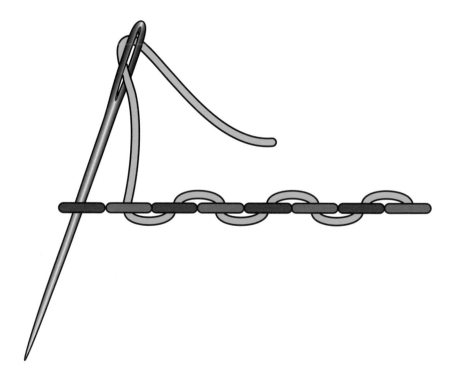

Threaded Back Stitch

After working a length of back stitch, work a second color of thread in and out of the stitching similar to the threaded running stitch. You can work the threaded pass through a single row of back stitch or through multiple rows to create a wider band of stitching.

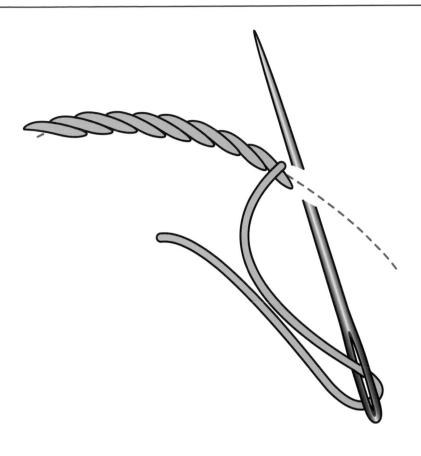

Stem Stitch

Stem stitch is a basic stitch that produces a solid line of stitching. This stitch can used to outline shapes or as stems and tendrils in a project. The stitch is worked by taking tiny stitches backwards along the outline of the shape. The working thread is held below the needle, with each stitch slightly covering the previous stitch. Rows of closely spaced stem stitch can also be used as a filling stitch. A similar stitch called the outline stitch is worked in the same manner, but with the thread held above the needle. The stitches can be used interchangeably.

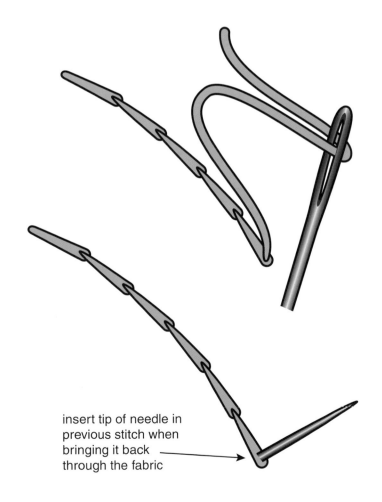

insert tip of needle in previous stitch when bringing it back through the fabric

Split Stitch

Split stitch forms a solid line of stitching and can be used to outline a shape, as stems and tendrils, or to outline an area that will be filled with satin stitch. To work the stitch, bring your needle up through the fabric at the starting point and take a stitch forward. Bring the needle up through the fabric at the center of the stitch you just made, splitting the stitch before inserting the needle into the fabric again to make the second stitch.

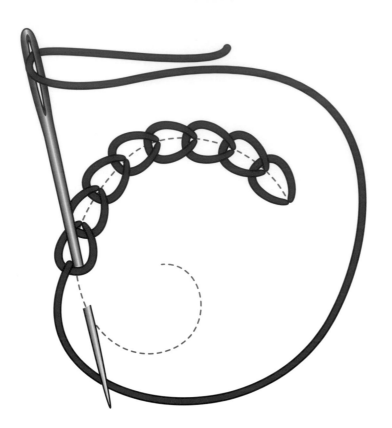

Chain Stitch

Chain stitch forms a thicker line of stitch with a decorative, chained effect. It can be used to outline shapes or as a filling by working closely spaced rows of stitching. The stitch is worked by forming a loop around the tip of the needle, with the needle insertion point in the same location as when you brought the needle up through the fabric. Each subsequent stitch starts inside of the previous stitch, forming a chain.

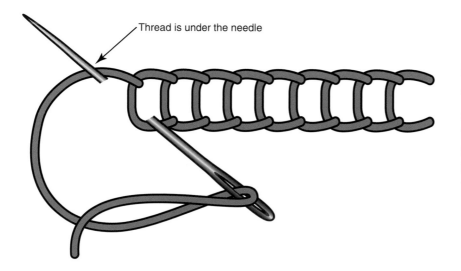

Thread is under the needle

Square Chain Stitch

This stitch is worked in the same manner as standard chain stitch, with the exception that the insertion point for the needle is a slight distance from the original entry point, giving the stitches a squared appearance.

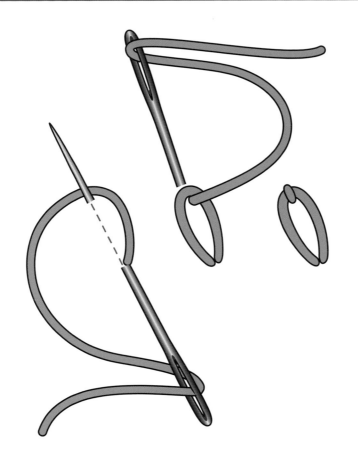

Detached Chain Stitch

Detached chain stitch is similar to chain stitch; however, instead of making a chain of multiple stitches, you make a single looped stitch, held in place with a small tacking stitch at the opposite end of the loop. Detached chain forms the basis of the lazy daisy stitch.

Lazy Daisy Stitch

The lazy daisy stitch is not a stitch per se, but instead is the name given to a group of detached chain stitches when they are worked in a flower pattern. Work just a few stitches to make a light, airy flower, or work the stitches densely packed to make a bolder bloom.

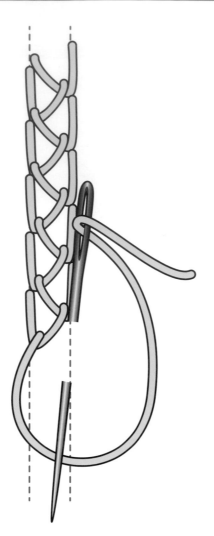

Double Chain Stitch

This stitch is worked similarly to a standard chain stitch. The difference is that instead of following a center line while stitching, you work along two parallel lines, giving the finished stitch a pretty zigzag effect.

Twisted Chain Stitch

This stitch is also worked similarly to regular chain stitch, with the original needle entry and exit point crossing each other, forming a very decorative twisted stitch.

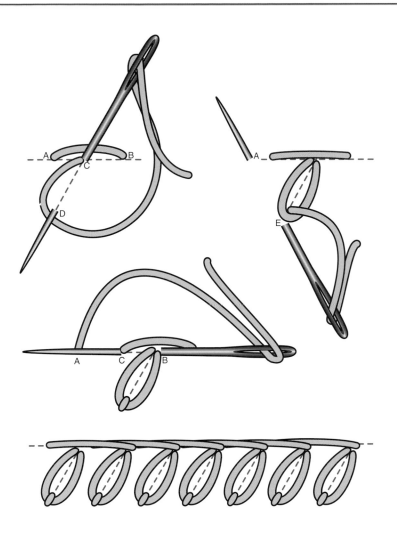

Chain Stitch Pendant

Sometimes called a petal stitch, or leafy chain, this stitch is actually worked with a combination of back stitch and detached chain stitch. The stitch can be worked to outline a basic shape, in rows, or alongside other stitches to form a decorative border.

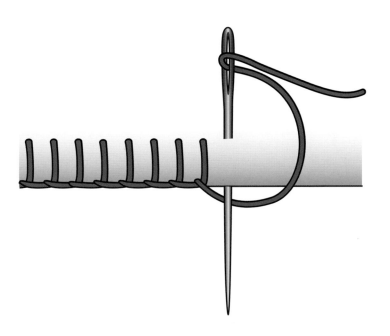

Blanket Stitch

Blanket stitch is used for working along the edges of the fabric: defining the perimeter with a decorative element, appliquéing fabric shapes to fabric, or outlining shapes in an embroidery pattern. The **L**-shaped stitch is easy to work, but should be evenly spaced and of equal lengths.

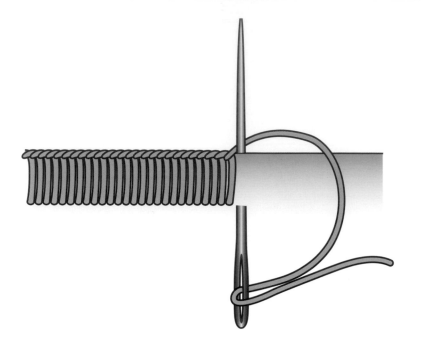

Buttonhole Stitch

Worked similarly to blanket stitch, but placed very close together, buttonhole stitch is used when a firm edge is needed, or when the fabric will be cut away from the opposite side of the looped edge, as it is for cutwork embroidery, or buttonholes, hence its name.

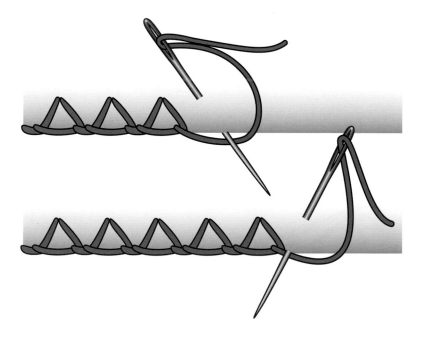

Closed Buttonhole Stitch

This stitch can be used to outline a shape or as a decorative, airy stitch along the edges of your fabric. The slanting stitches form a triangle design.

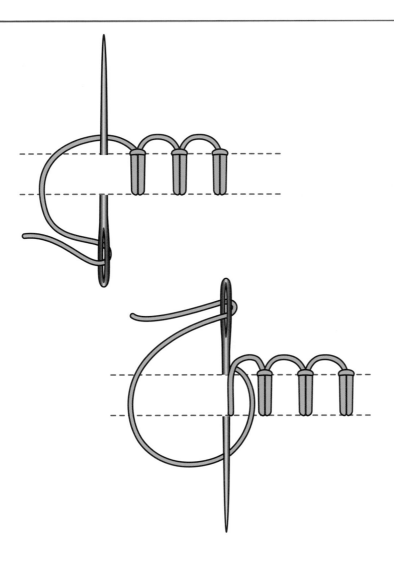

Up and Down Buttonhole Stitch

This stitch is best worked along a hemmed edge and can be a bit harder to master than other edging stitches, but is well worth the effort. The spacing between each double vertical stitch adds a pretty looped element to the edging.

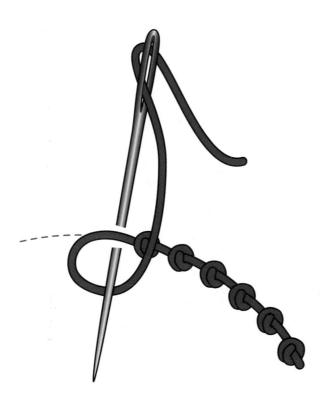

Coral Stitch

This stitch is made using small knots along the stitching line, creating a textured effect that can be used as an outline for embroidered shapes or as stems for flowers.

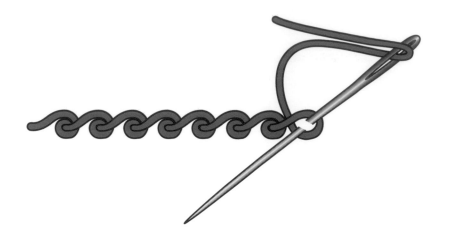

Scroll Stitch

The knots created along the stitching line using this stitch resemble scrolls. The stitch is worked by making a loop with the thread on the surface of the fabric and then taking a stitch through the loop. It can be used in rows and borders or to outline shapes.

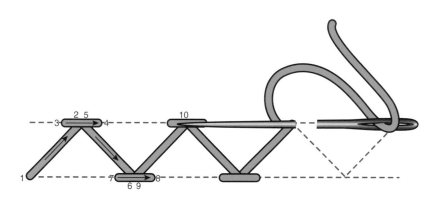

Chevron Stitch

The chevron stitch is best used in rows and borders and features zigzag stitch topped by a straight, horizontal stitch. It is easiest to work as a counted-thread stitch, but can also be used for surface embroidery by carefully marking the spacing on the fabric using a water-soluble, fabric-marking pen or pencil.

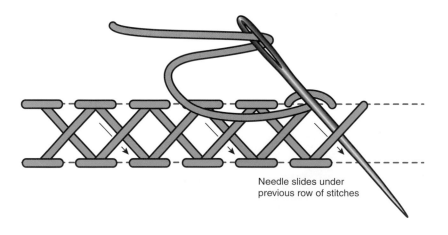

Needle slides under
previous row of stitches

Double Chevron Stitch

This stitch is worked in two passes. Work the first pass of chevron stitch in the first color. When working the second pass in the second color, slide the needle under the stitch worked in the previous pass when working the downward stitches.

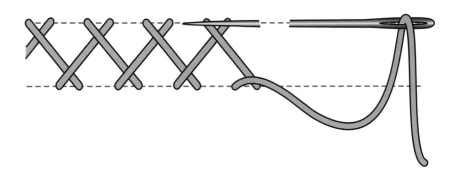

Herringbone Stitch

This decorative stitch forms overlapping zigzagging lines of stitching that are perfect for rows and borders or for outlining a shape. It is easiest to work as a counted-thread stitch, but can also be worked in a surface embroidery project by carefully spacing or premarking the stitches on the fabric. This stitch looks terrific with ribbon threaded through it.

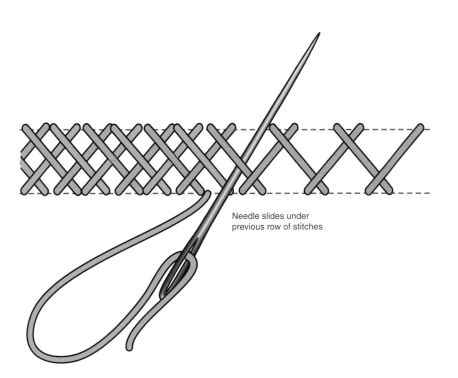

Needle slides under previous row of stitches

Double Herringbone Stitch

This stitch is worked in two passes of the herringbone stitch in two different colors. While working the second pass, the needle slides under the previous stitching when working an upwards stitch. Use this stitch in straight rows or borders.

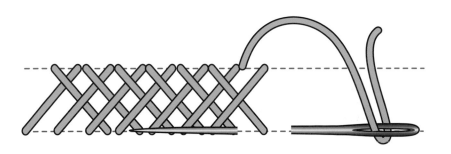

Closed Herringbone Stitch

This row or border stitch is a denser version of the herringbone stitch, with the newest stitch worked through some of the same entry and exit holes as the previous stitches, creating a tighter-spaced stitch.

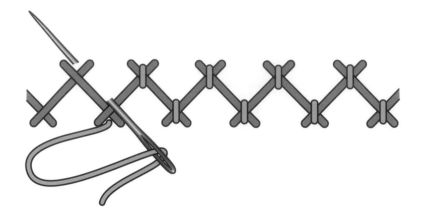

Tied Herringbone Stitch

This stitch can be worked as a row or border or as a decorative outline stitch. Work a row of herringbone stitch in the first color, followed by small tacking stitches over each stitch intersection using a second color of thread.

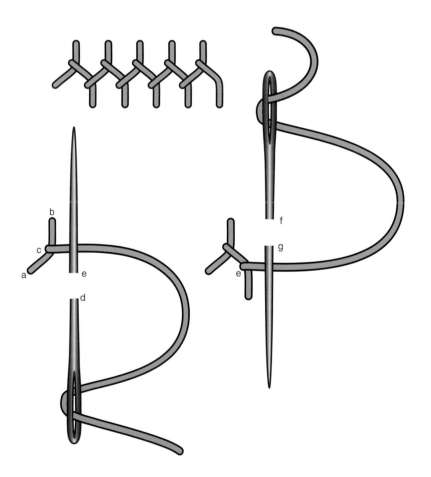

Open Cretan Stitch

Working this highly textured stitch is a bit like working the blanket stitch in opposing directions. It's best used when worked as a row or border, but can be used to outline shapes if carefully spaced.

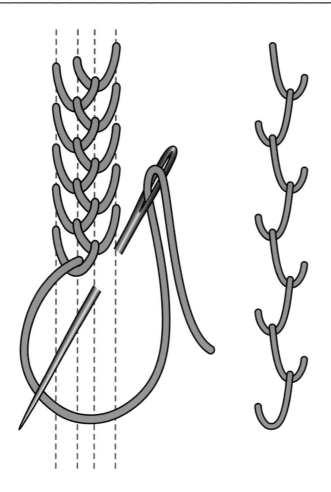

Feather Stitch

This versatile, textured stitch is the master of illusion. When worked closed spaced, the stitch makes a thicker border or band. Worked father apart, the stitch is open, airy, and thin. Use this stitch in borders and rows or to outline shapes. It also mimics thorny stems and seaweed beautifully.

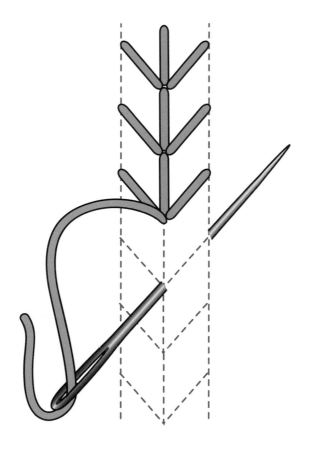

Fern Stitch

This easy, textured stitch is worked in three straight stitches, with the insertion point for each stitch at the base of each three-stitch group. These groups are worked repeatedly along the line of stitching. Be sure to space and work each group uniformly for the best results.

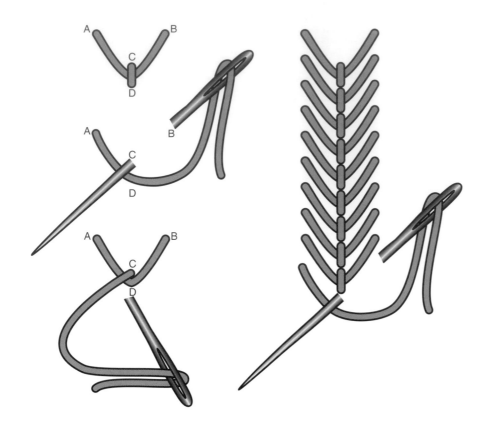

Fly Stitch

The fly stitch can be worked along a straight or curved line and is heavily textured. The stitch is worked by making a horizontal stitch that is tacked in place with a small, vertical stitch worked slightly below it, forming a **V**-shape.

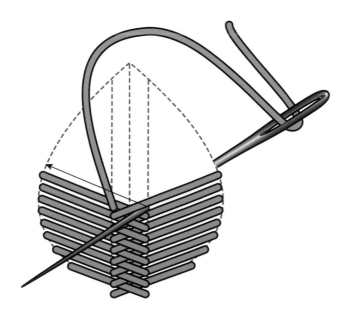

Leaf Stitch

This stitch gets its name because it is commonly used to fill a leaf shape in an embroidery pattern. The criss-crossing motion of the stitching forms a raised center band in the leaf, mimicking the center vein. The stitch is worked from the stem end to the top of the leaf, from the opposite side of the center of the leaf outwards at an angle.

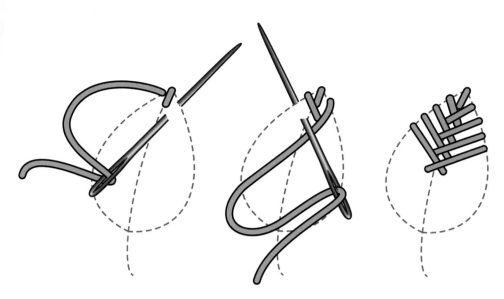

Fishbone Stitch

This stitch is worked in the opposite direction as the leaf stitch, starting at the top of the leaf and working back to the stem. This produces a leaf with two definite halves, without the raised center vein.

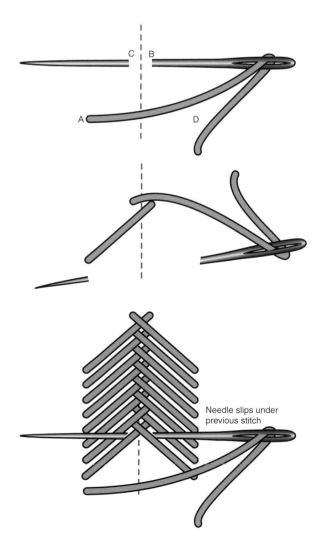

Needle slips under previous stitch

Van Dyke Stitch

This stitch is worked similarly to the fishbone stitch, but as a border or band. It is best to work this stitch in straight lines only, as curved lines can be difficult to maneuver.

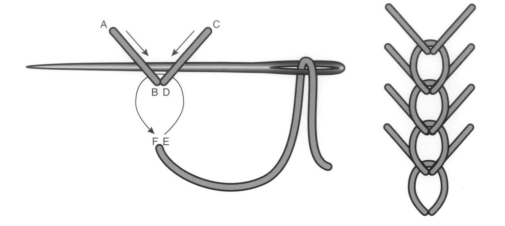

Wheatear Stitch

The wheatear stitch can be worked as a textured border or band in a straight line or along a curve. Each stitch is composed of two diagonal stitches facing opposite directions that meet at their bottom, threaded with a loop similar to a detached chain stitch.

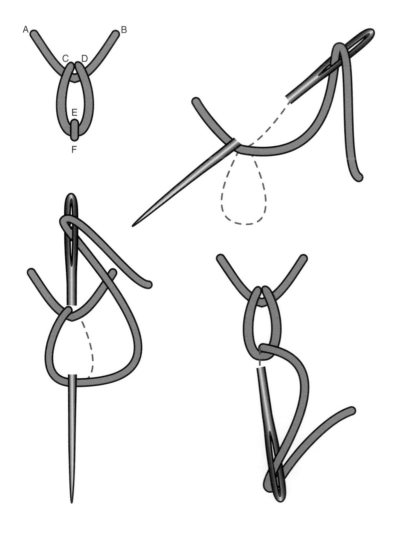

Wheatear Stitch Detached

The wheatear can also be worked as a single stitch and used on its own or as a scatter filling. Instead of having two diagonal stitches that meet in the center, a single horizontal stitch is made, followed by a looped stitch spaced slightly below the horizontal stitch. Because the stitch resembles the head of a steer, it is often called the *tete de boeuf* stitch.

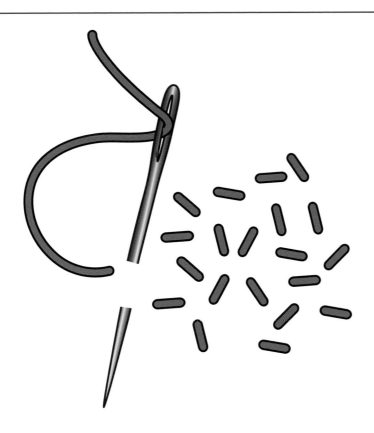

Seed Stitch

The seed stitch is a light, airy scatter filling, made by working small straight stitches randomly in an area to fill it.

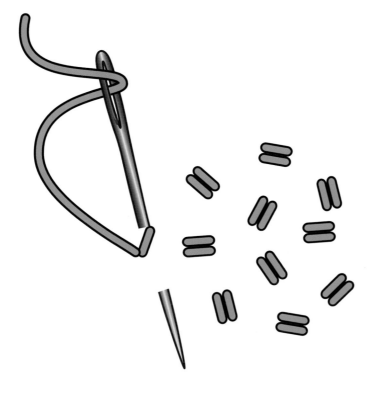

Double Seed Stitch

Also a scatter filling, this stitch is worked similar to the seed stitch, but uses two stitches placed side-by-side, creating a two-stitch group. The double seed stitch makes for a more pronounced, heavier filling than the single seed stitch.

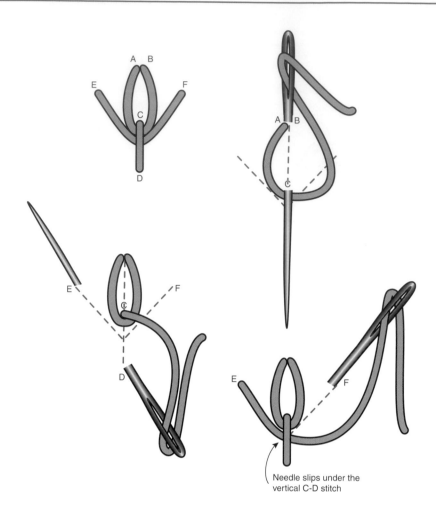

Needle slips under the
vertical C-D stitch

Tulip Stitch

The tulip stitch is a single stitch that
can be used individually, worked in
rows, or used as a scattered filling
stitch. To make this stitch, work a
single detached chain stitched with
an extra-long tacking stitch (the tacking stitch becomes the stem of the
flower). Then, work a horizontal
stitch under the chain stitch and
through the tacking stitch to make
the leaves.

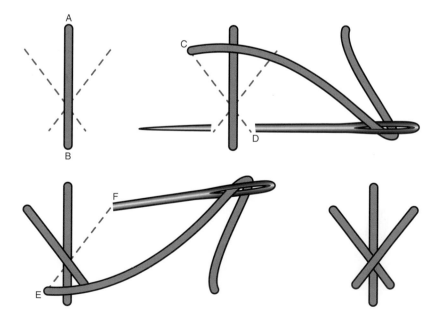

Ermine Stitch

The ermine stitch can also be used
individually, worked in rows, or used
as a scattered filling stitch. It's made
from a vertical straight stitch crossed
by elongated diagonal stitches.

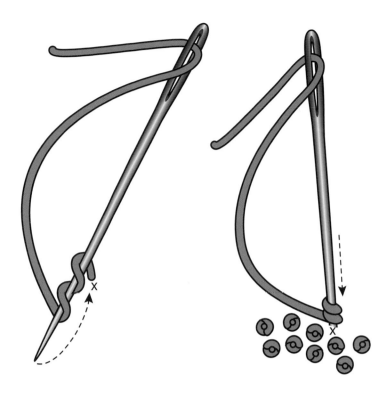

French Knot

French knots are easy to work once you've practiced them. To work a knot, bring the needle up through the fabric and wrap the working thread around the needle twice. Insert the needle back into the fabric very close to, but *not* in the same hole as you came out of, and pull the thread through, guiding it with your opposite hand as it passes through the fabric. Do not wrap too tightly or you'll have a difficult time pulling the needle through the knot. The thread should be against the needle, but not snug or tight. If your knot pulls through to the other side when working the stitch, try loosening the wrap a bit, and make sure you're not going down into the same hole. You will need a bridge to hold the knot on the surface; usually just a fiber or two in the fabric will suffice.

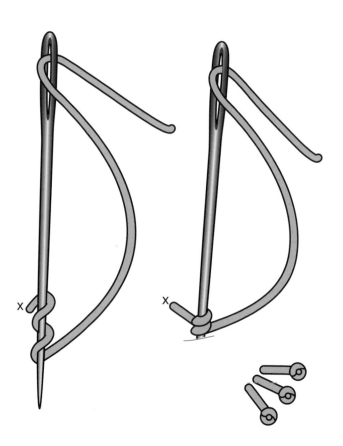

French Knot with Tail

Work this stitch the same as you would the standard French knot, with the exception of inserting the needle a longer distance from the original hole, giving the finished stitch its characteristic tail. This stitch is terrific for making individual small flowers or flower stamens.

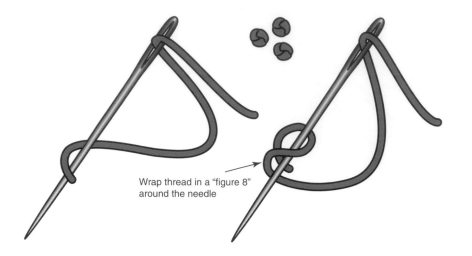

Wrap thread in a "figure 8"
around the needle

Colonial Knot

The colonial knot is typically used for candlewick projects and forms a sturdy knot that is easier to work in chunkier threads (like candlewicking thread) than a French knot. The working thread is wrapped around the needle in a figure-eight before the needle is inserted back into the fabric near the original hole.

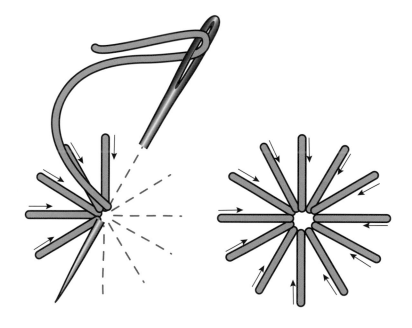

Algerian Eyelet

An Algerian eyelet can be worked in rows and borders, stitched around the edges of shapes, used to make a small flower or star, or used as a scattered filling stitch. The rays of the stitch are worked from the outside towards the center, leaving a small hole, or *eye*, in the center. Any number of rays can be used depending on the desired effect.

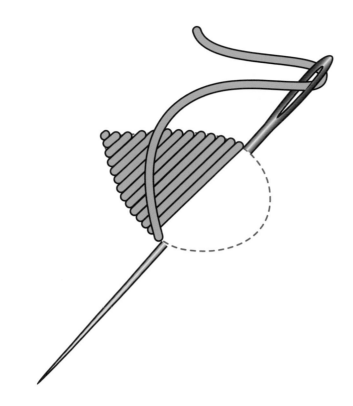

Satin Stitch Flat

Flat satin stitch is worked by laying down straight stitches without any padding or outlining. This stitch can be difficult to taper around a curve.

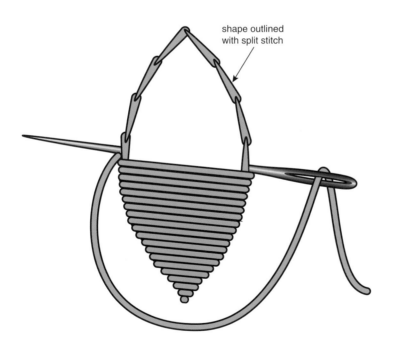

shape outlined with split stitch

Satin Stitch Outlined

Use the outlined satin stitch when working around curves, because it will help you maintain a smooth, rounded edge by forming a guideline to follow. The outlining can be worked in split stitch or back stitch, which gives the edges a bit of lift.

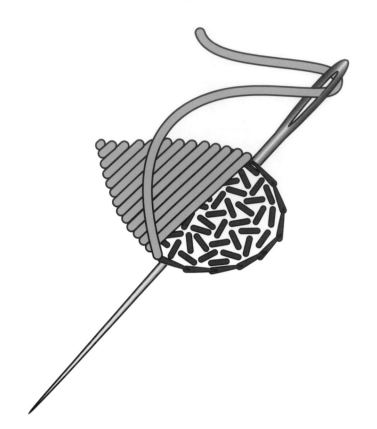

Padded Satin Stitch

After working an outline of back stitch or split stitch, fill the shape with seed stitches. Work the satin stitches over the filling stitches to create a raised shape. Other options for padded satin stitch include layers of satin stitch or working the satin stitches over felt or fusible interfacing the has been cut to shape and tacked or fused to the background fabric.

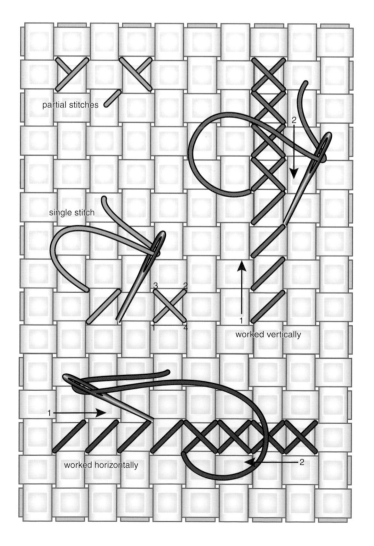

partial stitches

single stitch

worked vertically

worked horizontally

Cross Stitch

Cross stitch can be worked as a counted stitch over a single square on Aida fabric (shown here) or over two threads when using an even-weave fabric. It can also be used in a surface embroidery project by carefully marking the surface of the fabric. Each stitch comprises two di-agonal stitches that cross in the center. They can be worked individually or in vertical and horizontal rows. Keep the stitches uniform by making sure the top stitch always crosses in the same direction, from upper left to lower right. When working a counted chart, you may also find that partial stitches are used, usually a half or quarter stitch.

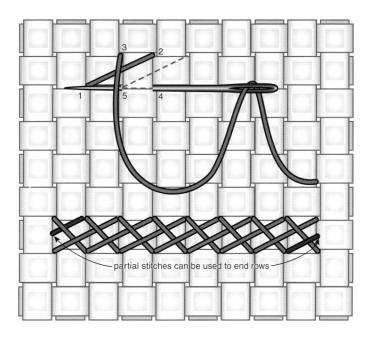

partial stitches can be used to end rows

Long Arm Cross Stitch

Long arm cross stitch is used to make borders and rows and can be worked as a counted stitch, or by carefully spacing the stitches in a surface embroidery project. The first part of the stitch is worked the double width of a single cross stitch, while the second part of the stitch is worked over a single width.

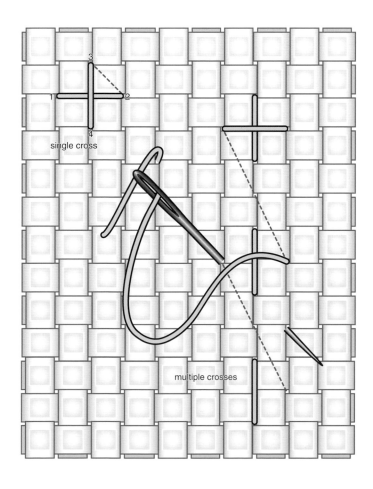

single cross

multiple crosses

Upright Cross Stitch

Upright cross stitches are worked with a vertical straight stitch crossed by a horizontal straight stitch and can be worked on surface embroidery or counted-thread projects. When worked on Aida fabric (shown here), the upright cross is worked over two intersections in the fabric.

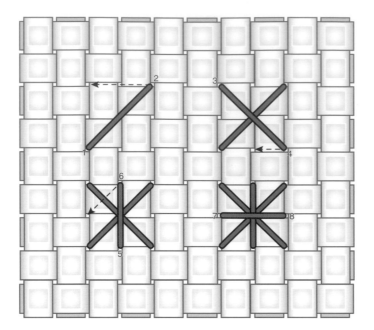

Double Cross Stitch/Cross Stitch Star

A double cross stitch is composed of a single, standard cross stitch followed by an upright cross stitch. This stitch can be used to make stars, fillings, and decorative borders or bands in a project.

Zigzag Stitch

The zigzag stitch is used to create decorative bands and borders in a project and is worked in two passes. The first pass is worked from right to left, working a vertical stitch followed by a diagonal stitch across the row. The second pass is worked in the opposite direction.

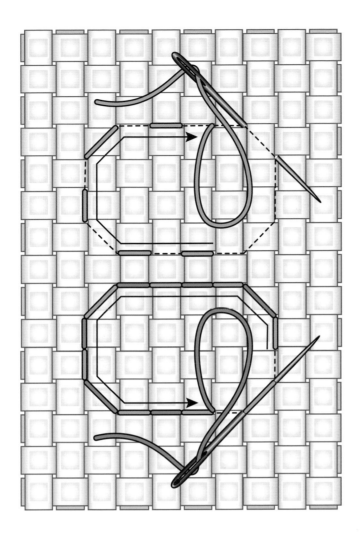

Holbein Stitch

The Holbein stitch is used to create a narrow line of stitch that looks the same on both sides of the fabric. Work Holbein stitch in two passes, similar to the double running stitch.

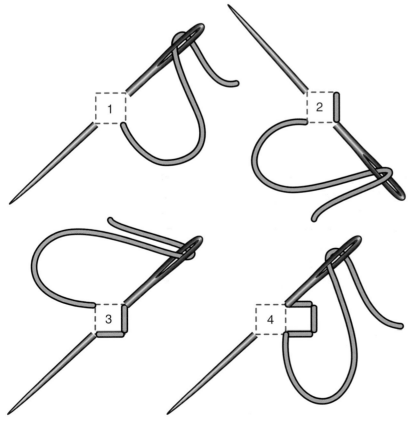

Four-Sided Stitch

This stitch is used to create small squares side-by-side, which can be used for borders and bands in a counted-thread project.

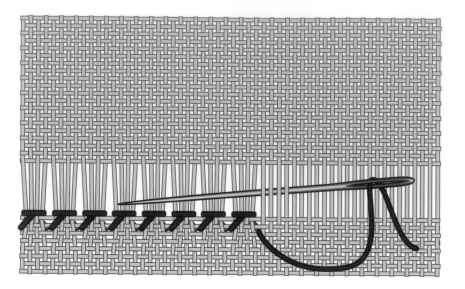

Hem Stitch

The hem stitch is used to secure groups of thread in a counted-thread project. It's used along openwork bands or along hems and fringed edges. To work the stitch, remove the required number of threads from the area. Then, thread a needle with either matching or colored thread and work the stitch around groups of two or more vertical threads in the open area. In this example the stitch is worked around groups of four vertical threads. Between each group, work a stitch through two horizontal threads to secure that group.

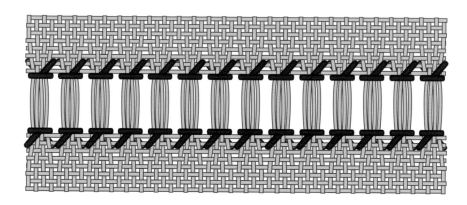

Ladder Stitch

The ladder stitch is worked by pulling out the required number of horizontal threads and then working the hem stitch on each side of the opening, using the same threads in the upper and lower bundles. The bundles of stitches resemble the rungs of a ladder, which gives the stitch its name.

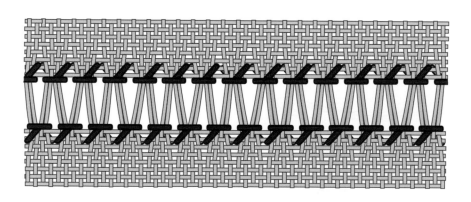

Serpentine Stitch

The serpentine stitch is worked similarly to the ladder stitch, except that the bundles of threads are split when working the upper and lower hem stitch areas.

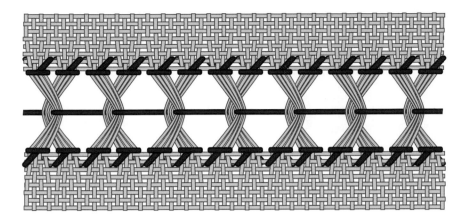

Twisted Border Stitch

This stitch is worked after a row of ladder stitch has been completed. A second thread is then worked along the center of the open band, twisting the bundles into a crisscross. This stitch looks really pretty when worked along a towel edge.

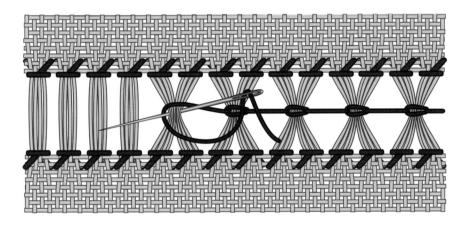

Knotted Border Stitch

This stitch is also worked after a row of ladder stitch has been completed. A second thread is then worked along the center of the open band, pulling two bundles of thread together and securing them with a knot.

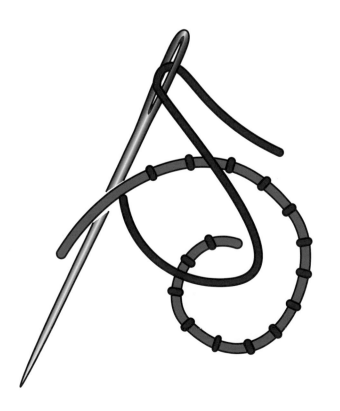

Couching

Couching is used to attach thick, wired, or decorative threads to the surface of the fabric. These types of threads are too thick to sew directly into place and are instead applied to the surface of the fabric. Couching should be done with a thin thread that is similar in color to the thicker thread being couched in place. Attach the thread to the fabric by bringing the needle with the thin thread up through the fabric, over the thicker thread, and down again near the originating hold, tacking the thicker thread into place.

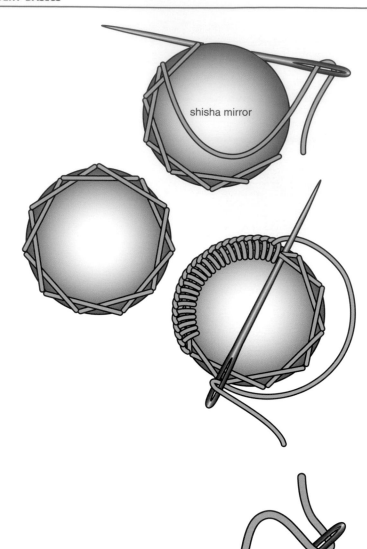

Applying Shisha Mirror

Shisha mirrors are attached by working straight tacking stitches around the edge of the mirror to secure it into place. Buttonhole stitch is then worked around the edges, on top of the mirror, to conceal the tacking stitches.

Whip Stitch

Whip stitch is used to secure two edges of fabric together or to attach trims to the edge of a finished project. Using a diagonal stitch, the thread is run up through the fabric and down again over the edges of the fabric.

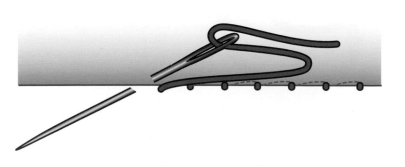

Invisible Stitch

This stitch is used to secure one layer of fabric to another with stitches that are nearly invisible and is commonly used to secure appliqués in place. The stitch is worked by taking a small tacking through the two layers of fabric and then running the needle through the space between the layers before exiting to take another stitch through both layers of the fabric.

Embroidery Projects

ere you will find an assortment of projects you can make using basic embroidery supplies and the stitches from the previous chapter. The projects are divided into two types: Projects 1 through 11 are Surface Embroidery, in which the thread sits on top of the fabric, and Projects 12 through 17 are Counted Thread, featuring designs using cross stitch and other techniques in which counting the threads in the fabric is required. Refer to the alphabetical index of stitches on page 106 to find the page numbers of any stitches you will use for the projects.

The colors and stitches recommended in many of the projects are merely suggestions. Feel free to change the stitches and colors or to use the motifs in a different way, such as on ready-made items you may have on hand. In fact, using embroidery is a great way to dress up an otherwise bland premade or purchased item.

Surface Embroidery Projects

48 Tutti-Frutti Three-Piece Kitchen Towel Set

51 Martini Cocktail Napkins

53 Embroidered Bag with Shisha Mirrors

56 Summer Lavender Two-Piece Pillowcase Set

58 Chain Stitch Blossoms Pillow Top

61 Alphabet Sampler in Surface Stitches with Matching Needle Case

66 Freestyle Embroidered Purse

68 Monogram with Padded Satin Stitch

71 Owl Pincushion

74 Owl Tablet Cover

76 Happy Halloween Framed Redwork

Counted-Thread Embroidery Projects

79 Italian Cross-Stitch Sampler with Pin Roll and Scissor Fob

85 Assisi-Style Tissue Holder

89 Drawn Thread Square Doily

92 Flower Basket Journal

95 Cross-Stitch Snowflake Ornaments

97 Blackwork Mini-Sampler

PROJECT 1
Tutti-Frutti Three-Piece Kitchen Towel Set

Stitch a set of embroidered kitchen towels in three tempting, luscious fruit colors. Work an apple for a vivid green towel, a lemon for a sunny yellow, and a ripe melon for the orange. Or, select colors of floss to match your own towels.

The fruits are worked separately from the towels on pieces of linen fabric. The finished design is then trimmed to size, hemmed, and attached to the towels as an appliqué.

The stitches used in this project include stem stitch, running stitch, French knots, padded satin stitch, and blanket stitch.

MATERIALS

- A prepurchased kitchen towel for each design

- An 8 x 10-inch piece of white 36-count linen for each towel (I used Edinburgh from Zweigart)

- 6-strand embroidery floss in colors bright green, yellow, and orange (DMC colors 907, 973, and 922 were used in the samples)

- A spool of white all-purpose sewing thread

- Size 8 embroidery needle

DIRECTIONS

1. Fold each rectangle of linen into quarters to find the center. Transfer the design to the center of each linen rectangle using your favorite transfer technique (see page 16).

2. *Apple Towel:* Using three strands of floss in bright green, embroider the apple and leaf shapes in stem stitch. Work the seed in the center of the apple in padded satin stitch using three strands of floss. Using two strands of floss, embroider the apple details (indicated by dashed lines on the pattern) in running stitch.

3. *Lemon Towel:* Using three strands of the yellow floss, embroider the lemon and leaf shapes in stem stitch. Also using three strands, embroider the seed in the lemon wedge using a single detached chain stitch. Using two strands of floss, work the details in the skin of the lemon (indicated by small dots on the pattern) in French knots, wrapping the thread once around the needle for each knot.

4. *Melon Towel:* Using three strands of the orange floss, embroider the melon and wedge shapes in stem stitch. Also using three strands of floss, embroider the seeds in the melon wedge using detached chain stitches. Using two strands of the floss, embroider the skin details in the melon (indicated by small dots on the pattern) in French knots, wrapping the thread once around the needle for each knot. Also using two strands, embroider the area under the seeds in running stitch.

5. *Make the appliqué:* Trim the linen fabrics down so that they measure 5 x 6½ inches, making sure you keep the fruit embroidery centered as you trim. Turn under the edges of the fabric ¼ inch along all four sides and baste the folded hem in place with large stitches using all-purpose thread (this basting will be removed later).

6. Center the appliqués on each towel, spacing them about 1½ inches from the lower edge. Baste the appliqués in place using the all-purpose thread.

7. Using two strands of the same floss used in each fruit, attach the appliqués to the towels using the blanket stitch, making certain each stitch penetrates not only the appliqué, but the towel underneath as well.

8. After all of the appliqués have been attached using the blanket stitch, remove the basting threads from the appliqués. The towels are now ready for use.

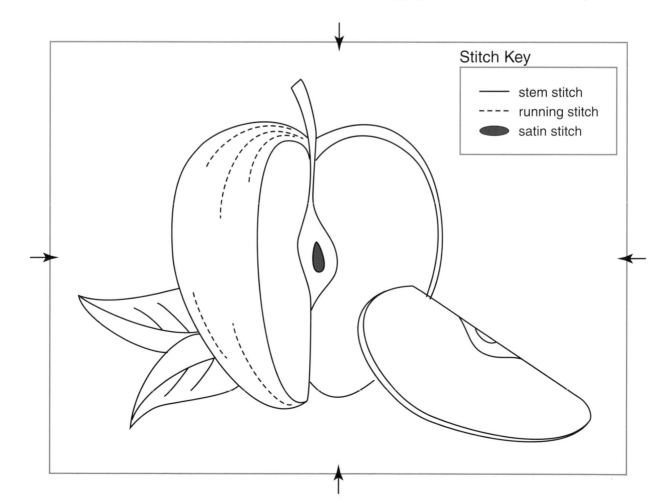

Stitch Key

——— stem stitch

- - - - running stitch

⬤ satin stitch

Stitch Key

— stem stitch
••• French knots
detached chain

Stitch Key

— stem stitch
- - - running stitch
••• French knots
detached chain

Martini Cocktail Napkins

Create a *stir* at your next party by serving your guests their martini accompanied by a hip, hand-embroidered cocktail napkin. Each napkin features a single cocktail glass embroidered with basic stitches, including the back stitch, satin stitch, and French knots.

Arrange the design facing a slightly different direction to keep a light-hearted "one martini, two martini, three martini, floor" vibe going. Just for fun, I've also included alternate patterns in case lemon drops or a glass of wine are more your style.

The finished embroidery design fits nicely into the corner of a 5-inch cocktail napkin.

MATERIALS

- 5-inch cocktail napkins in a plainweave or evenweave fabric

- 6-strand embroidery floss in colors dark gray, green, orange-red, and golden brown (DMC colors 844, 470, 782, and 349 were used in the sample)

- Size 8 embroidery needle

DIRECTIONS

1. Transfer the design to a corner on each cocktail napkin using your favorite transfer technique.

2. Embroider the outline of the martini glass using three strands of dark gray 6-strand floss in your needle using back stitch. Embroider the bottom of the martini glass bowl area using two strands of the same floss in back stitch.

3. Using the satin stitch, embroider the olive in the glass using two strands of the green floss. Work a French knot on each olive using three strands of the red floss for the pimiento.

4. Embroider the toothpick using three strands of the golden brown floss in back stitch.

TIP: You can embroider the design on ready-made cocktail napkins or make your own. I've made my own by working a ½-inch hem stitched self-fringe around a 5-inch square made from a 28-count evenweave fabric.

PROJECT 3
Embroidered Bag with Shisha Mirrors

Shisha are small glass mirrors or shiny objects that are applied to fabrics, adding shimmer and interest to an embroidery project. This style of embroidery was popular in Persia, where it was known as *shisheh*, and once used mica flakes instead of glass. It is now most commonly seen in India.

Mirrors for shisha are available in different sizes. In this project I have used ¾-inch mirrors as the centers of flowers placed on the corners of a square embroidered base, which is folded to create a pouch. Starting with smaller mirrors that are easier to attach is the best way to try this beautiful type of embroidery.

Note: Shisha mirrors should not be confused with paillettes, a type of large sequin, which are made from acrylic or metal and have a small hole in them for attaching to fabric. These holes are often visible in the finished project if paillettes are used. Shisha mirrors do not have holes.

Embroidery stitches used in this project include closed buttonhole stitch (used to secure the mirrors), feather stitch, coral stitch, back stitch, detached chain stitch, and French knots.

The finished bag is 6 x 6 inches square.

53

MATERIALS

- 12 x 12-inch piece of 28-count antique white evenweave fabric for embroidery (I used Monaco from CharlesCraft.)

- 12 x 12-inch piece of plainweave solid or print fabric for the lining

- DMC size 5 pearl cotton in 799 medium delft blue, 554 light violet, 604 light cranberry, 471 light avocado green, 369 very light pistachio green, and 676 light old gold

- White all-purpose sewing thread to match the embroidery fabric

- 36-inch length of narrow cording

- Size 7 embroidery needle

- Clear plastic snap, ribbon, or extra cording for closure

1/2 of bag pattern

DIRECTIONS

1. Fold the square of fabric into quarters to mark the vertical and horizontal centers. Using a water-soluble fabric marking pen (do not use heat transfer or other permanent markings in this design), mark the embroidery design and the triangle outlines on the fabric. Because of its size, only half of the pattern is given, but since the design is symmetrical, you can trace the second side by flipping the fabric 180 degrees.

2. Attach the shisha mirrors first, using the shisha directions. Refer to the stitch guide to embroider the remaining design.

3. Trim the excess fabric to within ½ inch of the triangle borders to make a ½-inch seam allowance.

4. Lay the embroidered fabric face down on the lining fabric, having the right sides of both fabrics facing. Using a ½-inch seam allowance and the all-purpose thread, stitch the two fabric pieces together by hand or machine, leaving a 2-inch opening along one side edge for turning.

5. Clip the corners of the fabric close to—but not through—the stitching and turn the material right side out. Hand-stitch the turning opening closed and press the finished fabric square.

6. Fold three corners of the fabric square towards the center, making a pocket. Whip-stitch the three corners together to secure it, using the all-purpose embroidery thread. The stitches should be very small and inconspicuous. The fourth corner will be the flap of the bag.

7. Hand-stitch the length of cording around the edges of the bag starting at one side of the flap area. When you return to your starting point, make a loop from the remaining cording and attach to the opposite side of the flap to make the handle.

8. Stitch a snap, ribbon, extra cording, or other closure to the flap and pocket area and the bag is ready to use.

Stitch Key

ᔓᔓ	Feather stitch
- - - -	Back stitch
∾∾∾	Coral stitch
∘	French knot
↶	Detached chain

Summer Lavender
Two-Piece Pillowcase Set

SKILL LEVEL: **Beginner**

Embroidery is a great way to dress up even the simplest things, and these pillowcases are a great example of spiffing up an otherwise boring item. You can embroider the design along the fold-over flap of a flat sheet as well, creating a custom set.

The repeating floral design is worked in four different stitches including the stem stitch, detached chain stitch, straight stitch, and French knots. The coordinating accent pillowcase is worked in laced running stitch.

The embroidery design can be made to fit any size of sheet set by repeating the simple pattern.

MATERIALS

- Set of pillowcases in white (or the entire set of sheets)
- DMC 6-strand embroidery floss in colors 986 very dark forest green, 989 forest green, 209 dark lavender, 327 dark violet, 791 very dark cornflower blue, and 729 medium old gold
- Size 8 embroidery needle

DIRECTIONS

1. Transfer the design to the pillowcases using your favorite transfer techniques. Both temporary and permanent transfers will work in this project.

2. Use three strands of the 6-strand floss throughout the project.

3. Embroider the stems and tendrils in stem stitch using the medium green floss. The leaves at the bottom of each flower cluster are worked in detached chain using the dark green floss.

4. Referring to the color key, work the flower clusters in detached chain stitches using the medium and dark lavender flosses.

5. Work the flower tips in dark purple using three straight stitches that meet at the base, topped with a French knot in gold.

6. The second pillowcase is worked in three bands of laced running stitch using medium green and medium lavender.

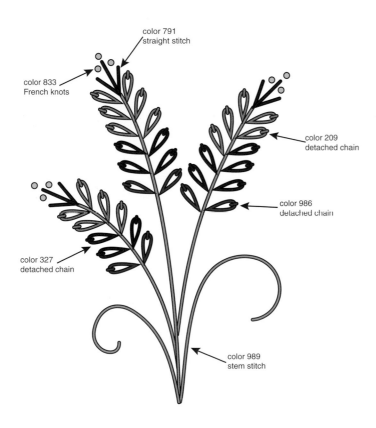

color 791
straight stitch

color 833
French knots

color 209
detached chain

color 986
detached chain

color 327
detached chain

color 989
stem stitch

PROJECT 5
Chain Stitch Blossoms Pillow Top

SKILL LEVEL: **Beginner**

Chain stitches are used as both outlines and a filling in this bold, bright beauty, framed with double running stitch. Size 5 pearl cotton was used to work the entire design, resulting in thick stitches that suit the simple pattern well. If you prefer to use embroidery floss, use three strands of floss in your needle for similar results.

The finished size is approximately 14 x 14 inches.

MATERIALS

- 16 x 16-inch piece of heavier-weight evenweave or plainweave fabric, such as linen or twill

- 14 x 14-inch piece of backing fabric to coordinate with the thread colors

- DMC size 5 pearl cotton in colors 907 parrot green, 742 tangerine light, 352 coral light, 817 coral red very dark, 3345 hunter green dark, and 725 topaz

- Size 3 embroidery needle, polyester fiberfill for stuffing or a 14-inch pillowform

DIRECTIONS

1. Using a water-soluble fabric marking pen, lay out a grid of nine 4 x 4-inch squares in the center of the fabric. Mark the flower design in the center of each square.

2. Work the flower designs from the center outwards, using randomly chosen colors of the pearl cotton. All of the embroidery is worked in chain stitch, first outlining the shape and then filling in the two center circles and the outer petal band. The inner petal band is not filled, but is instead outlined with chain stitch.

3. The fillings in my sample contain three to four rounds of chain stitch filling. It is not necessary to work the rounds of chain stitch too close together, because this stitch is thicker and fills an area quickly.

4. Once the flowers have been stitched, work the double running stitch in two colors of the pearl cotton along all of the grid markings. Wash the pillow to remove the markings and press from the back side of the fabric, so you don't flatten the chain stitching.

5. To finish the pillow, trim the fabric down to 14 x 14 inches (1 inch from the outer grid lines) and complete the pillow, referring to the pillow finishing directions on page 15.

PROJECT 6

Alphabet Sampler in Surface Stitches with Matching Needle Case

Reminiscent of surface embroidery patterns from the 1930s and '40s, this simple sampler has a funky, retro look perfect for a home decorated in hip, mid-century modern style, and it fits a standard 8 x 10-inch frame. Use bright floral colors like I've done here, or change the colors to suit your own décor.

The optional needle case can be used to store embroidery and hand-sewing needles, or use the sampler in the nursery and store diaper pins in the case.

Sampler

MATERIALS

- 16 x 32-inch piece of ecru plainweave fabric

- 2 skeins each of DMC embroidery floss in colors 907 parrot green, 742 tangerine light, 553 violet, 899 rose medium, and 3766 peacock blue light

- Size 8 embroidery needle

- 8 x 10-inch frame and framing supplies

8 x 10

DIRECTIONS

1. Fold the piece of sampler fabric into quarters and mark the center with a water-soluble marking pen. Trace the design onto the center of the fabric using the same pen.

2. Using three strands of the 6-strand embroidery floss, work the design, referring to the sampler color key. The stems, tendrils, and alphabet are worked in stem stitch, flowers in lazy daisy, and flower centers and accent dots in French knots.

3. Wash the piece to remove the markings and frame the sampler, referring to the framing directions on page 101.

Color Key

Needle Case

MATERIALS

- ⅓ yard ecru plainweave fabric and leftover threads from the sampler

- Acid-free press board

- Scrap of wool felt

- 1 yard of narrow corded trim

DIRECTIONS

1. Cut one 8 x 10-inch piece of fabric. Mark the needle case design on the piece as shown.

2. Following the needle case color key, work the design. After completing the design, wash and press the fabric. Referring to the figure, cut out the 7½ x 5-inch rectangle from the fabric.

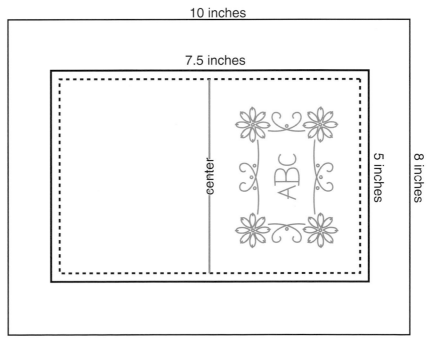

Mark embroidery and cutting lines (solid lines) on the 8 x 10-inch piece of fabric. Cut out a 5 x 7½-inch fabric section after completing the embroidery.

3. Cut two 4 x 5 pieces of fabric from the ⅓-yard cut. Cut two 3½ x 4½-inch rectangles from the press board.

4 inches

5 inches

Cut 2 from fabric

3.25 inches

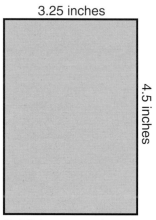

4.5 inches

Cut 2 from pressboard

4. Fold under ¼ inch along one long edge of each of the 4 x 5 pieces of fabric. Place these rectangles on top of the embroidered section, having the right sides facing and the folded edges meeting at the center. Stitch around all four sides of the fabric using a ¼-inch seam allowance and matching sewing thread. Clip the corners to reduce bulk.

Fold along one long edge of each lining piece

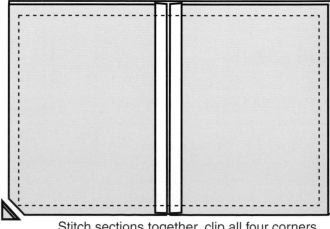

Stitch sections together, clip all four corners.

5. Turn the resulting envelope rightside out through the opening at the center of the lining. Insert one of the pieces of pressboard into each side of the lining. Hand stitch the center opening closed using the whip stitch or invisible stitch.

6. Hand-stitch the corded trim (you can make your own, see page 102) to the outside edges and across the center fold of the needle case using a whip stitch. Tack leftover lengths to the center front and center back to make ties for keeping the needle case securely closed.

7. From the felt, cut a 3 x 4-inch rectangle using pinking shears and hand-stitch it to the inside of the needle case.

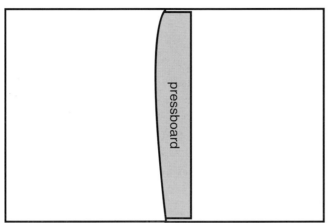

Insert pressboard into each pocket

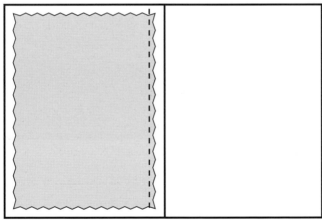

Stitch felt in place by hand

PROJECT 7
Freestyle Embroidered Purse

Freestyle embroidery is a term used to describe any type of surface embroidery in which no actual pattern is used. The embroiderer simply chooses the stitch and threads he or she feels work best in a particular area.

This type of embroidery is perfect for embellishing plain, ordinary objects and is a lot of fun. Let your imagination dictate your next stitch!

The finished size depends entirely on the size of the ready-made purse.

MATERIALS

- Ready-made fabric purse or any size of type
- Coordinating colors of 6-strand embroidery floss
- Size 8 embroidery needle

DIRECTIONS

1. Using two strands of floss in the needle, embroider random stems and tendrils using the back. The stems can cross the body of the purse and pockets by stitching only through the top layer of fabric. Add leaves worked in detached chain stitch, and flowers using both the detached chain stitch and the lazy daisy stitch.

2. Flower centers are worked in French knots. French knots with tails and groups of individual French knots can be used for smaller flowers. In the figures shown here, you can see several of the random flower groupings that were used in the purse.

3. I've also accented the upper area of the flap and the snap area with a few cross stitches to add interest to the piece.

Monogram with Padded Satin Stitch

SKILL LEVEL: **Beginner**

Centuries ago, linens were among the treasures of a household and were very expensive. The items were monogrammed to identify their owners when they were sent out for cleaning, because most well-to-do families had others do their laundry for them.

Monogramming is still popular, especially on bridal gifts, blankets, and towels. In this project, the finished monogram is used as a box lid. You can also transform it into a pillow front or tote pocket, or frame it and enjoy it as art.

The simple alphabet can be enlarged or reduced to be used on virtually any type of monogramming project and filled with any number of stitches and stitch combinations.

In this example, I've used classic, padded satin stitch surrounded by a frame of tied herringbone stitch.

The finished size of the embroidered area is approximately 3 inches square.

MATERIALS

- 10 x 10-inch piece of 32-count linen evenweave fabric

- Embroidery floss in two colors (I have used DMC floss in colors 3820 Dark Straw and 3817 Light Celadon Green in the sample)

- Size 8 embroidery needle

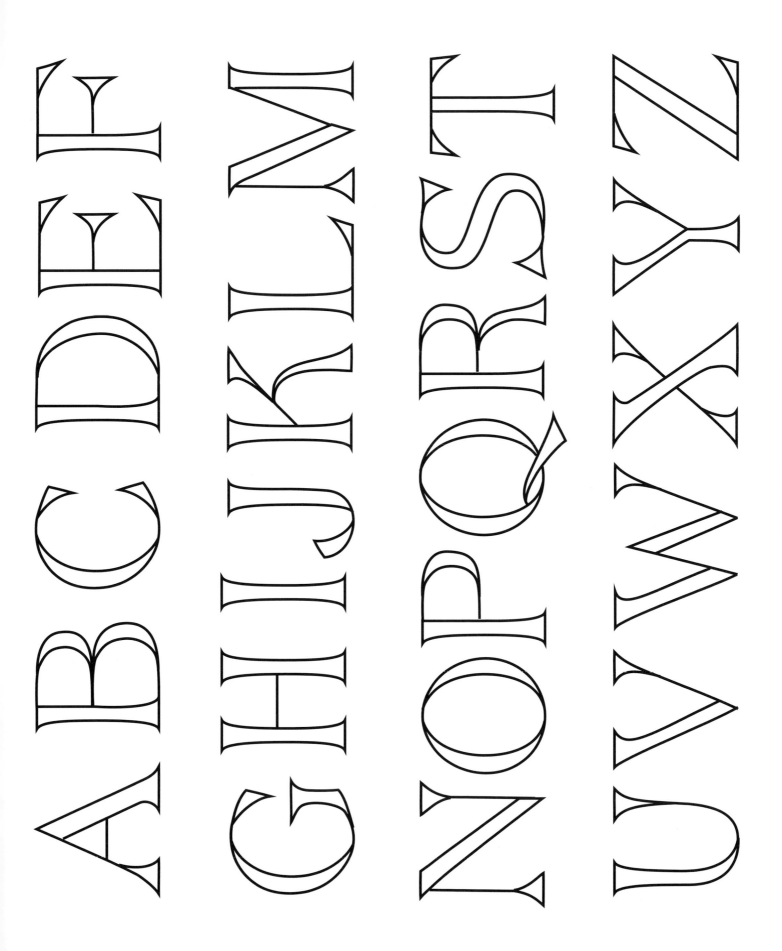

DIRECTIONS

1. Fold the square of fabric in quarters to locate and mark the center. Using a water-soluble fabric marking pen, trace the outer border area and monogram in the center of the fabric. I've provided an entire alphabet. Feel free to substitute another alphabet if you wish.

2. Using the main color of floss, work the monogrammed letter in the center of the design using the padded satin stitch, stitching with 2 strands of floss in the needle. I have padded the stitch in the sample with seed stitch, but you can also use running stitches, or concentric bands of chain, or stem stitch to pad the area.

3. Work the border in the tied herringbone stitch using 3 strands of the main color of floss in the needle. The second color of floss is used to "tie" the herringbone stitch at the intersections.

PROJECT 9
Owl Pincushion

SKILL LEVEL: **Beginner**

This adorable—and useful—project can be made quickly and is a nice gift for a stitching friend. The entire design is worked using all six strands of floss, with the exception of the blanket stitch edging, which uses three strands.

The finished size is approximately 5 inches high by 7 inches wide.

MATERIALS

- Wool felt in white, yellow, green, and rust

- DMC embroidery floss in colors 743 medium yellow, 518 light wedgewood blue, 907 light parrot green, 469 avocado green, and 921 copper

- Size 7 embroidery needle

- 2⅜-inch white buttons

- Small amount of polyester fiberfill for stuffing

- Scrap of ribbon

DIRECTIONS

1. Using a water-soluble fabric marking pen, mark the owl body on the rust felt, the beak on the yellow felt, the eyes on the green felt, and the heart-shaped belly on the white felt. On the remaining rust felt mark two sets of wings.

2. Embroider the designs on the belly using all six strands of the floss in stem, detached chain, and French knots.

3. Cut out the belly shape and appliqué it to the owl body by stitching around the edges of the belly using all six strands of the yellow floss.

4. Appliqué the eyes in place in the same manner using the blue thread. Appliqué the beak in place using the copper thread. Attach a button to each eye area using the blue floss. Work a cluster of three detached chain stitches above each eye and two detached chain stitches below the eyes.

5. Cut the owl body from the felt, and then cut a second body shape from the felt. Place the two shapes together, wrong sides facing, and pin the two layers together. Work the blanket stitch around the edges of the body using three strands of floss. When you are within 1½ inches of your starting point, stuff the body lightly with fiberfill. Continue stitching around the body shape.

6. Embroider a cluster of three detached chain stitches in the green floss and a French knot in the blue floss on a pair of the wings. Cut out the embroidered wings and the second set of wings (these will be the wing backings). Stitch an embroidered wing to a backing section using the blanket stitch in three strands of floss as you did for the body, but do not stuff them.

7. Tack a wing to the back of the owl body at each side, stitching them in place using the invisible stitch with a single strand of the copper floss.

8. Tack a length of ribbon to the top of the owl for hanging (optional) to complete the project.

PROJECT 10
Owl Tablet Cover

Build your stitch repertoire while making a pouch to protect your expensive tablet, e-reader, or smartphone. The project requires just a few basic sewing supplies in addition to the embroidery materials.

The actual size of the finished pouch depends on the size of your equipment, and these instructions make it easy to create a custom-sized case for virtually any flat electronic device. The adorable owl design is featured on both the front and back sides of the pouch.

MATERIALS

- ¼ to ½ yard heavy woven fabric in solid tan for the pouch and a lightweight printed fabric for the lining

- DMC embroidery floss in colors 743 medium yellow, 518 light wedgewood blue, 907 light parrot green, 469 avocado green, and 921 copper

- Size 7 embroidery needle

- 4 ⅜-inch rust or copper-colored buttons

- Scrap of sew-in hook and loop tape (Velcro™)

DIRECTIONS

1. Measure the height and width of your device. Now, add 2 inches to this measurement. For example, if your device is 8 x 10 inches, your measurement will be 10 x 12 inches.

2. Mark two rectangles using this measurement on the heavier-weight fabric using a water-soluble fabric marking pen or permanent pen (if the fabric is dark).

3. Transfer the design to the two marked rectangles, spacing the image at least 2 inches from the side and bottom edges.

Pattern

4. Using the stitch key, embroider the design on both of the rectangles using three strands of floss of all of the embroidery. The stitches used in this project include the outline stitch, running stitch, seed stitch, padded satin stitch, French knot, and detached chain stitch.

5. Cut the two embroidered rectangles from the fabric. Cut a 3-inch flap the same width as the short end of the rectangles. If desired, round off the corners along one longer side.

   Cut the exact same pieces from the lighter-weight lining fabric (two rectangles and a flap).

6. Stitch the two embroidered rectangles together on a sewing machine. With their right sides facing, stitch along the bottom and side edges using a ⅝-inch seam allowance. The top edge will remain unstitched.

7. Repeat with the lighter-weight fabric for the lining, leaving the top edge unstitched, but also leave a 2-inch opening along the bottom short edge for turning. Turn the lining section right-side-out.

8. To make the flap, place the lining and heavy fabric flaps together with their right sides facing. Stitch around the front and side edges of the flap, leaving the back edge unstitched. Clip the corners or curves to eliminate some of the fabric bulk and turn the flap right side out. Press the flap and edge-stitch around all four sides of the flap, ⅛ inch from the edges.

9. Pin the flap to the open end of the embroidered pouch section, aligning the sides of the flap with the seams. Baste the flap in place using a ¼-inch seam allowance.

10. Place the lining inside the embroidered pouch, having their right sides facing (this is why you turned the lining right-side out). Stitch around the open edge of the pouch using a ⅝-inch seam allowance. Turn the bag rightside-out through the opening left in the bottom edge of the lining. Hand-stitch the opening in the bottom edge of the lining closed using the whip stitch.

11. Tuck the lining into the pouch and press. Edge-stitch around the pouch opening to help keep the lining inside the bag. Stitch the hook and loop tape in place to keep the flap closed. Stitch the buttons to the eye areas to complete the project.

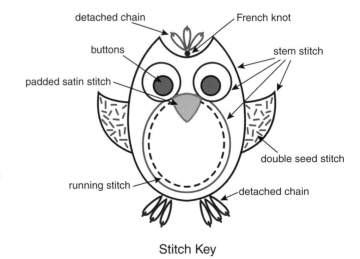

Stitch Key

Happy Halloween Framed Redwork

Redwork, a popular form of embroidery during the late 1880s through early 1920s, uses red thread on white or natural fabric. It's very popular with both embroiderers and quilters alike.

Stitch this jovial bunch of pumpkins to welcome guests during Halloween.

The pattern is worked in three basic embroidery stitches—stem stitch, back stitch, and French knots using embroidery floss.

The finished size fits a 5 x 12 ready-made frame.

MATERIALS

- 11 x 18-inch piece of 32-count evenweave linen in natural or antique white

- 6-strand embroidery floss in color 816 or a similar red

- Size 8 embroidery needle

- Frame and framing supplies

DIRECTIONS

1. Transfer the design to the pillowcases using your favorite transfer techniques. Because of its size, the design is given in two pieces. Line up the center line for each side when tracing on the fabric. Both temporary and permanent transfers will work in this project, as it will be easy to cover the lines with the red thread.

2. Referring to the stitch key, use two strands of the 6-strand floss to embroider the solid lines in stem stitch and the dots in French knots. Use a single strand to embroider the dashed lines in running stitch.

3. When the embroidery has been completed, mount the piece to a backing and place it in the frame. Refer to the framing directions on page 101. Tip: A ready-made photo frame meant to hold two 3½ x 5 inch photos fits the design perfectly. Discard the matting and only use the frame.

Enlarge pattern 200%

DMC color #816

———————   work in stem stitch using 2 strands of floss

•   •   work in French knots using 2 strands of floss

- - - - - - - -   work in running stitch using a single strand of floss

PROJECT 12
Italian Cross-Stitch Sampler with Pin Roll and Scissor Fob

SKILL LEVEL: **Intermediate**

In this project, a script alphabet is accented with back stitching and surrounded by an ornate border. Matching accessories include a pincushion roll and a scissor fob, perfect for tucking into your workbasket. I've also included a graph for an optional bookmark!

Using just two shades of blue, the inspiration for this design comes from Italian Renaissance art. It reminds me of a romantic gondola trip along a canal in Venice enjoying a bottle of good wine and a chunk of cheese.

The finished sampler fits a 10 x 14-inch ready-made frame. The scissor fob measures 2 inches square and the pin roll is 7 inches in length, with a circumference of approximately 5 inches.

MATERIALS

- For the sampler: 16 x 24-inch piece of white 16-count Aida fabric

- For the accessories: 10 x 14-inch piece of white 16-count Aida fabric

- DMC 6-strand embroidery floss: 4 skeins of 3755 baby blue, and 3 skeins of 336 navy blue

- Size 8 embroidery needle

- White sewing thread, scraps of ribbon, polyester fiberfill

79

DIRECTIONS
Sampler

Because of the size of the sampler pattern, it is given in two sections; a left side and a right side.

1. Following the pattern and working from the center out, embroider the sampler on the larger piece of Aida fabric. All cross-stitch embroidery is worked using 2 strands of floss.

2. Work the back stitching in the border and the accents on the lettering using a single strand of floss (Holbein stitch may also be used, if preferred).

3. Frame the sampler as desired.

Pincushion Roll

1. Work the design onto the smaller piece of Aida cloth, spacing it 4 inches from the edges of the fabric.

2. Cut out the pin roll. There should be 3 inches of unstitched fabric along each of the two long sides and 1 inch of unstitched fabric extending from the short sides.

3. Fold the embroidered piece in half, right sides together, matching up the stitching along the sides with 1 inch of fabric extending.

4. Stitch by hand or machine along the doubled edge, using a 1-inch seam allowance. Turn the resulting tube right side out. Stuff firmly with the fiberfill and tie the ends closed with the ribbon to complete the roll.

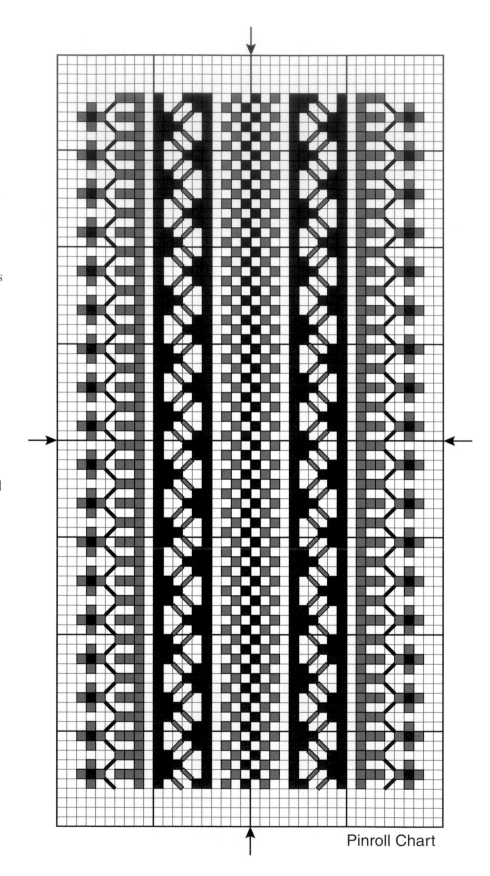

Pinroll Chart

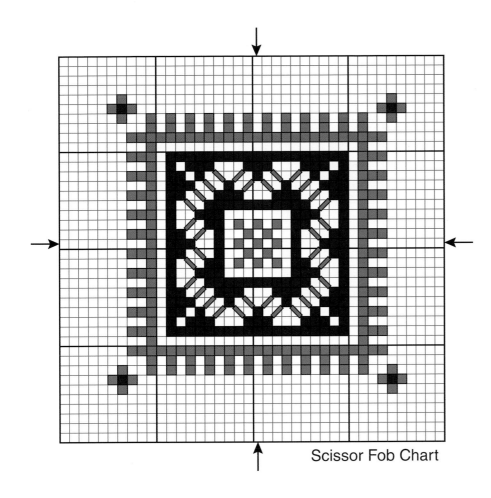

Scissor Fob Chart

Scissor Fob

1. Work the design on the remaining fabric scraps.

2. Cut out the design ¾ inch from the embroidered edges and finish as you would an ornament, stitching a backing and hanging loop to the piece.

Bookmark

Here is a graph for a bookmark using the patterns from this project.

Bookmark Chart

Assisi-Style Tissue Holder

Assisi embroidery is a form of cross-stitch where the background—instead of the motif—is filled with cross stitches and outlined with Holbein or back stitches. It's said to have originated in the town of Assisi in Perugia, Italy. Animals, florals, and geometric patterns are popular motifs, and in this example, a chain of leaves is used along each side of the opening of this easy-to-make tissue cover.

The finished holder fits a standard package of tissue, and is approximately 3 x 6 inches.

MATERIALS

- 14-count CharlesCraft Bright Ideas Aida in polar ice (bright blue), 10 x 10 inches

- Embroidery floss in blanc/white and 3845 medium turquoise

- Size 8 embroidery needle

- Sewing thread to match fabric

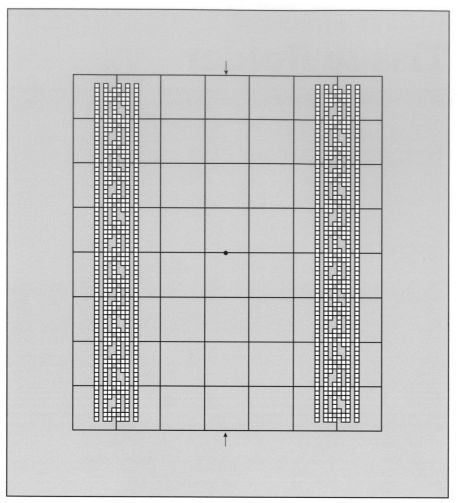

Work the design in the center of
the square of Aida. Trim to size
after completing the stitching.

DIRECTIONS

1. Fold the square of fabric in half
   and mark the center with a water-
   soluble fabric marker. Work the
   cross-stitch bands pattern on the
   fabric. The bands are spaced 20
   squares from the center of the
   fabric and 40 squares apart.

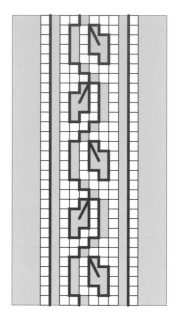

2. After working the cross-stitch,
   work the turquoise details in back
   stitch. You can see a detail of the
   backstitching in the diagram.

3. Trim the excess fabric so that
   the square measures 7 x 7 inches.
   Edge-finish all four sides by machine using an overcast stitch in
   matching sewing thread.

4. Fold the edges that run along the
   sides of the bands ¼ inch towards
   the wrong side. Tack the folded
   edge in place along the back side
   of the fabric using the whip stitch.

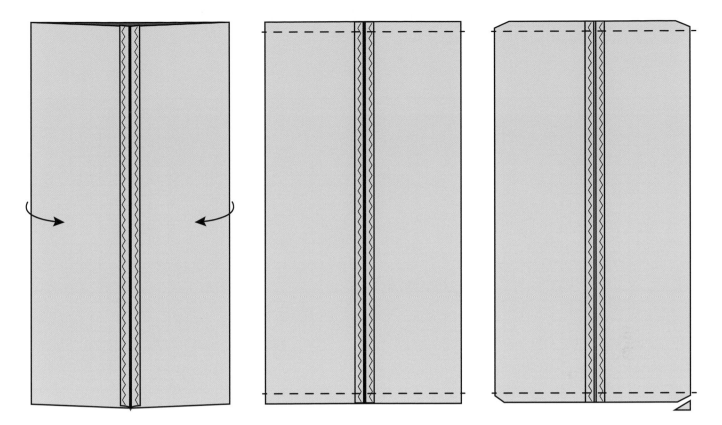

5. Fold the sides of the fabric towards the center so that they meet along your previously marked center line, with their right sides together. Machine-stitch across the top and bottom edges, ½ inch from the edge.

6. Clip the corners and turn the fabric envelope right
   side out. Press the piece and insert a packet of tissue
   to complete.

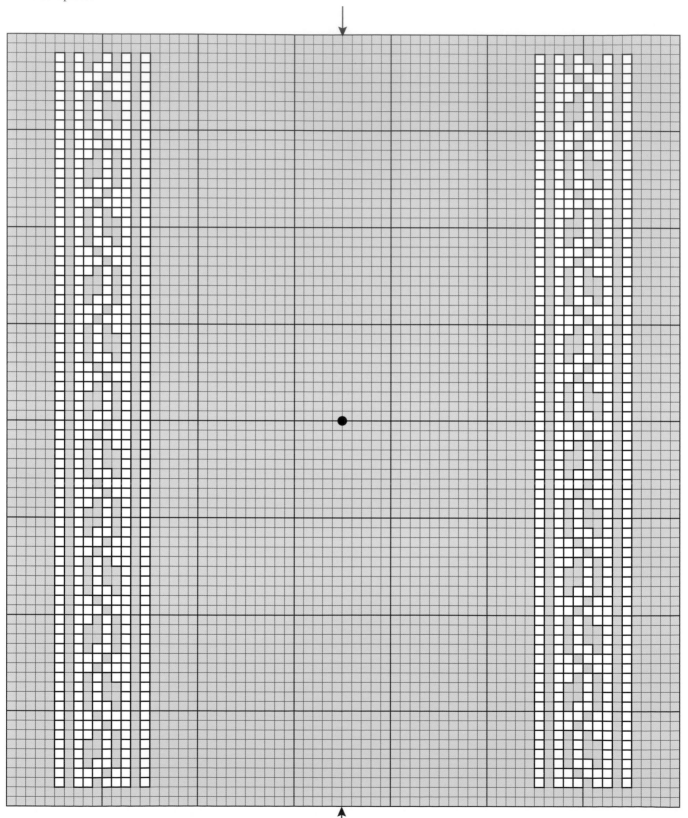

PROJECT 14
Drawn-Thread Square Doily

Learn to work the basic hem stitch as you create this pretty square doily. Enlarged versions of the Algerian eye stitch have been used as a filling in some of the squares, accented with counted straight stitch. The finished doily is 9 x 9 inches square.

MATERIALS

- 1 piece of off-white 32-count linen, 12 x 12 inches
- Cotton hand-sewing thread or embroidery floss to match the fabric
- 6-strand embroidery floss in colors very light avocado green and light old gold (DMC colors 676 and 471 were used in the samples)
- Size 8 embroidery needle

DIRECTIONS

1. Fold the square of embroidery fabric into quarters and place a small mark at the center using a water-soluble fabric marking pen. Starting from the center point and following the diagram, remove a single thread of fabric in each direction every 34 threads to make squares.

2. Work the hem stitch in a 2-thread group around every square using the hand-sewing thread (if using embroidery floss, use a single strand for all hemstitching). You will have 17 of the 2-thread groups. Work the hemstitch around the outside of the center area in 2-thread groups.

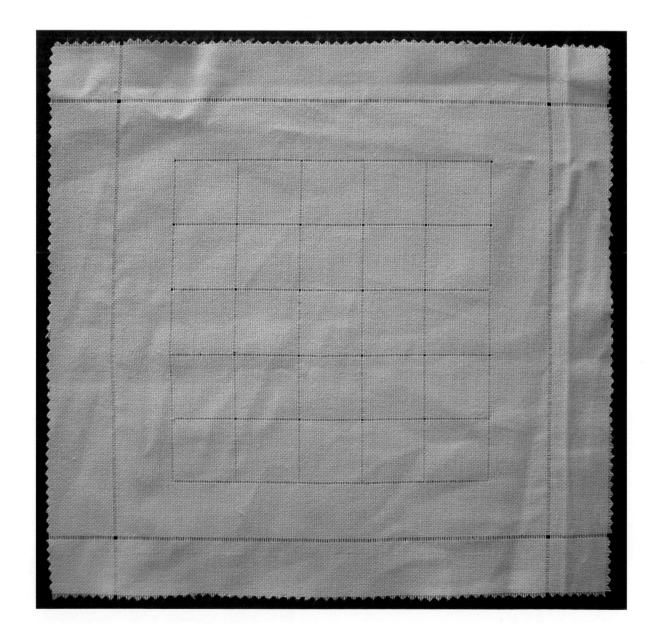

3. Remove a thread from the fabric 32 threads from the hemstitching around all 4 sides. Work the hemstitch around the inside edge of the gap in 2-thread groups.

4. Trim the fabric ¾ inch from the last line of hemstitching and make a self-fringe.

5. Work an enlarged Algerian eye embroidery in the squares indicated using 3 strands of floss. On the corner of each Algerian eye, work a group of 3 straight stitches as shown in the diagram using 2 strands of floss. Work a standard Algerian eye in 5 of the central squares to complete.

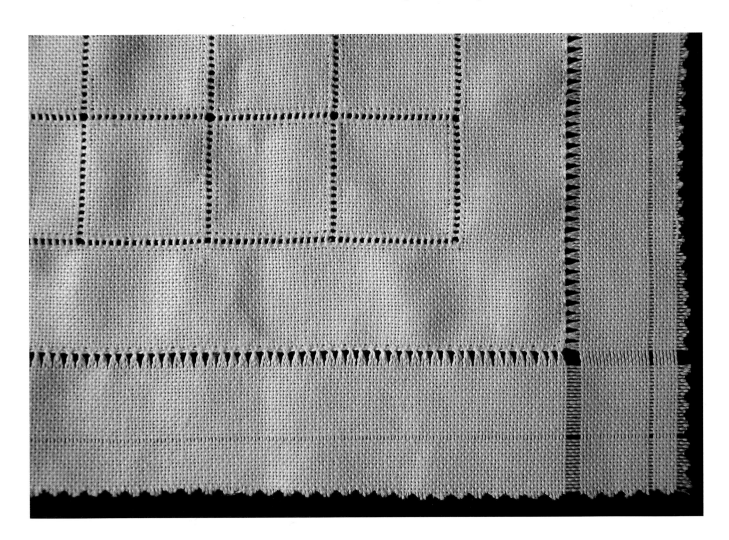

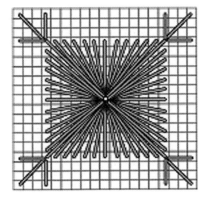

PROJECT 15
Flower Basket Journal

This pretty journal inspired by an antique crochet pattern graph makes a lovely gift for a new grandmother, a college graduate, or a dear friend's birthday. It's easy to select the paper colors and styles and change the colors of the flowers to suit the recipient. Each flower is made from just two shades of each color, and the basket is just a single color of floss. I have coordinated these colors with the papers.

The unfinished kraft paper journal that I used in the sample is available at most chain craft stores. If you can't find a journal the exact size as shown here, any unfinished paper size journal will do.

The finished embroidered area measures 4 inches square.

MATERIALS

- For the sampler: 10 x 10-inch piece of white 16-count Aida fabric

- DMC 6-strand embroidery floss, 1 skein each of 816 garnet, 3801 very dark melon, 327 dark violet, 209 dark lavender, 742 light tangerine, 744 pale yellow, 989 forest green, 986 very dark forest green, 436 tan

- Size 8 embroidery needle

- Blank, premade 7 x 6-inch paper journal; acid-free tag board measuring 4¼ x 4¼

- Decorative papers

- Glue stick

- Ribbon

- White sewing thread

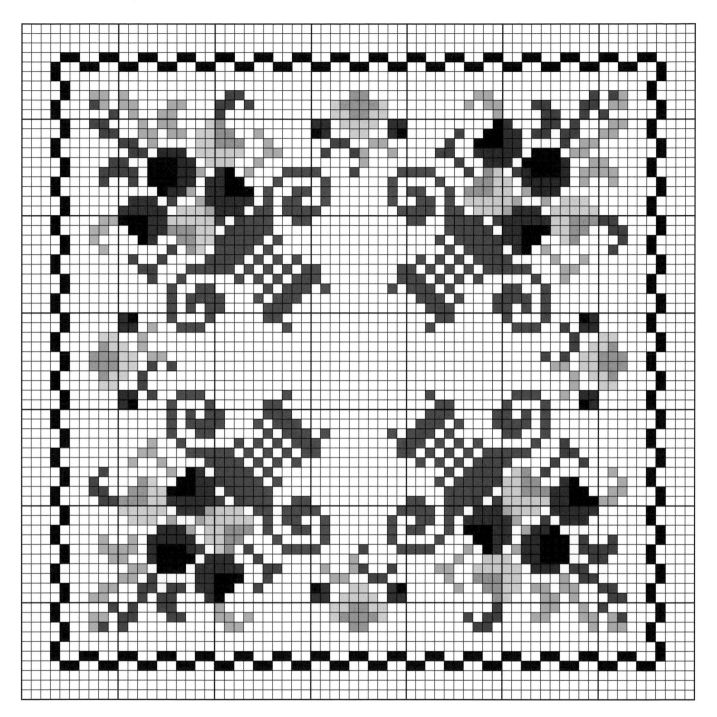

DIRECTIONS

1. Embroider the flower basket design using two strands of floss in the needle, following the charted pattern.

COLOR KEY

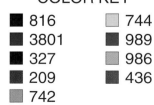

■	816	□	744
■	3801	■	989
■	327	■	986
■	209	■	436
■	742		

2. Trim the fabric so that it measures 6 x 6 inches, keeping the embroidered area centered. Attach the embroidery to the tab board, lacing it into place with the white sewing thread.

3. Cut paper to fit the journal, including extra to fold around the edges. Glue the papers in place. Cut additional accent papers for the spine or corner as desired and glue them in place. Add ribbon to the journal along the side, either gluing it in place or punching two holes and threading the ribbon through them.

4. Glue the embroidered emblem to the front of the journal to complete.

PROJECT 16
Cross-Stitch
̶ ̶lake Ornaments

-style ornaments in cross-stitch and ̶sing alternating colors of floss and ̶d white, but the designs would look ̶ blue and white, green and natural, or black and white. Choose your combination to suit your décor.

The finished size of each ornament is 3 inches square, excluding hanging loop.

MATERIALS

- 14-count Aida in white and red, 1 5 x 5-inch piece for each ornament

- 1 skein each of red and white six-strand embroidery floss to match the fabrics (DMC colors B5200 snow white and 304 red medium were used in the samples)

- Size 8 embroidery needle

DIRECTIONS

1. Locate the center of each square of Aida fabric and stitch the design, following the chart.

2. Work the design in white on the red fabric and the design in red on the white fabric. Use two strands of embroidery floss for all cross-stitch. Use a single strand of embroidery floss for the decorative scroll designs using either the Holbein stitch or back stitch.

3. Finish the squares as ornaments or holiday coasters.

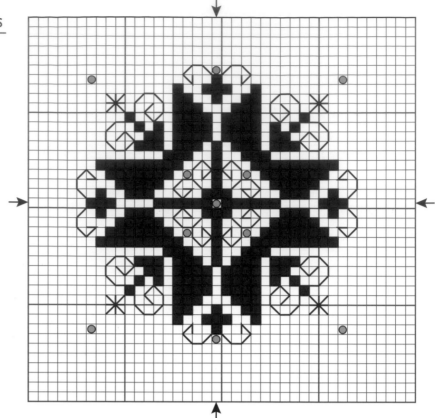

● Size 11/0 Glass Seed Bead
■ DMC Embroidery Floss Color 304 or Blanc (2 strands)
╲ DMC Embroidery Floss Color 304 or Blanc (1 strand)

Blackwork Mini-Sampler

Try your hand at traditional blackwork embroidery by stitching this square mini-sampler using back stitch or Holbein stitch. Blackwork was introduced to the fashionable ladies of the European courts by Catherine of Aragon, one of the unfortunate wives of Henry VIII.

This project is smaller and works up quickly, making it a terrific beginner's project. It's also a perfect piece to tuck into your handbag to work on while commuting or travelling.

The finished embroidered area measures 4½ inches square and fits a standard 5 x 5-inch frame.

MATERIALS

- 10 x 10-inch piece of 24-count evenweave fabric or 12-count Aida in a tan or natural color

- 2 skeins of black 6-strand embroidery floss

- Size 8 embroidery needle

DIRECTIONS

1. The entire design is worked in back stitch using 2 strands of embroidery floss. If thinner lines are preferred, use a single strand of floss.

2. Work each stitch in the design over 2 threads if using evenweave fabric or a single square if using Aida fabric.

3. The finished piece can be framed, like I've shown here, or used as the center motif of a pillow, or as a pocket for a tote or apron.

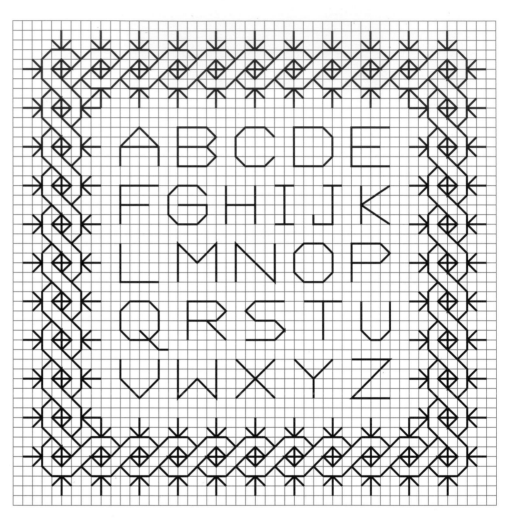

Thread used:
Wildflowers by Caron, color 196 sable

Finishing Touches

Here are some general sewing techniques that can be used to finish the projects in this book.

Blocking Basics

Sometimes an embroidered piece can seem a little out of kilter once it's finished. This often happens when a hoop isn't used. Squaring up a lopsided piece is very easy. Simply dampen the piece, pin it to a blocking board, and allow the piece to dry.

Blocking boards are fabric-covered, padded boards with a grid pattern on the fabric. Square the edges of the fabric with the grids, pulling and stretching as needed to align all four sides and securing them to the fabric grid with rust-proof T-pins.

Once the piece is dry it will stay squared and is ready to finish as framed art, a gift, or a home décor piece.

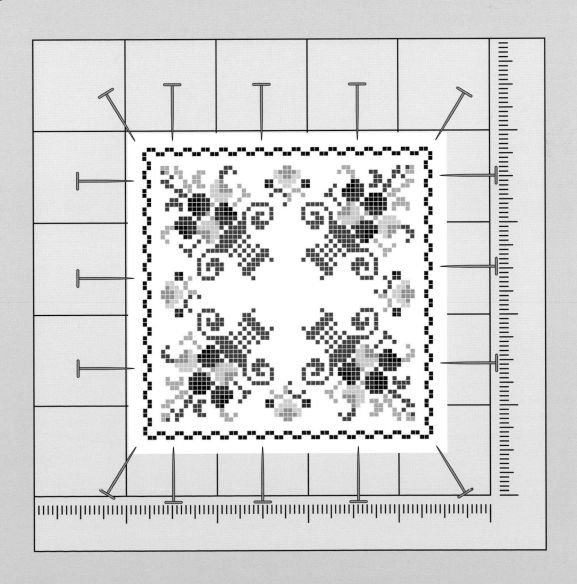

Making a Basic Pillow

Making a pillow is easy to do if you follow these basic steps. Pillows can be made of any size and shape, but when making pillows with corners, it's all about the corners. Sharp corners require some savvy snipping before turning rightside out.

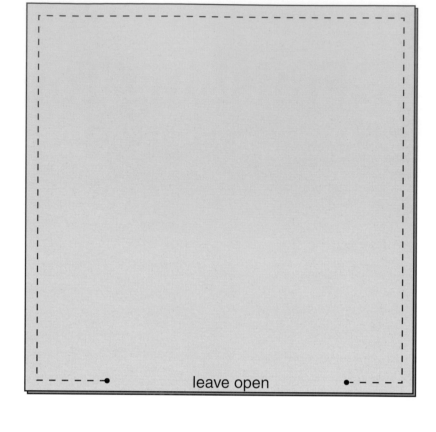

leave open

1. To make a pillow, cut the backing fabric the same size as the pillow top and place the pillow top and the backing fabric right-sides-together. Stitch around all four sides, leaving a large opening along the bottom edge. By leaving an opening rather than the entire bottom side unstitched, you'll have neater corners.

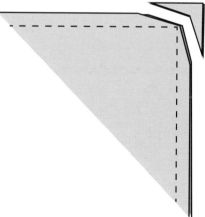

2. Next, carefully clip the excess fabric from the corners. Clip close to—but not through—the stitching, making angled cuts. Cutting about ⅛ inch from the stitching will suffice.

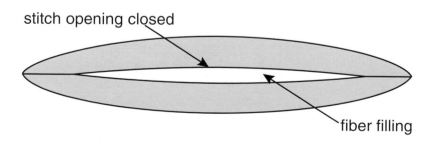

stitch opening closed

fiber filling

3. Turn the pillow covering rightside out and stuff with fiberfill, or insert a ready-made pillow form. Hand-stitch the opening closed using an invisible ladder stitch.

Mounting and Framing

Samplers and seasonal needlepoint designs look terrific framed, and care should be taken when mounting the piece to make certain it will last for generations and be removable for an occasional cleaning.

1. To frame a piece, edge-finish the fabric by working machine zigzag stitching around all four sides to prevent fraying. Then, fold under ½ inch of fabric around all four sides and secure the hem with machine stitching.

2. Next, center the piece on the backing board. The backing board can be tag board or foam-core board, but should be acid-free and archival quality. Regular tag board and foam-core board that is not acid-free will yellow over time, and that yellow will transfer to the fabric and ruin it.

3. After centering the item on the board, place a pin in each corner and at the centers of each side of the board to hold the fabric in position.

4. Lay the board face-down on your work surface and use strong sewing thread to lace the fabric to the backing board as shown. Lace the short sides first, followed by the long sides.

5. Remove the pins from the sides and corners and the item is ready to place in the frame.

TIP: Fabric needs to breathe to stay healthy. Therefore, use spacers between the embroidered piece and the glass, or eliminate the glass altogether.

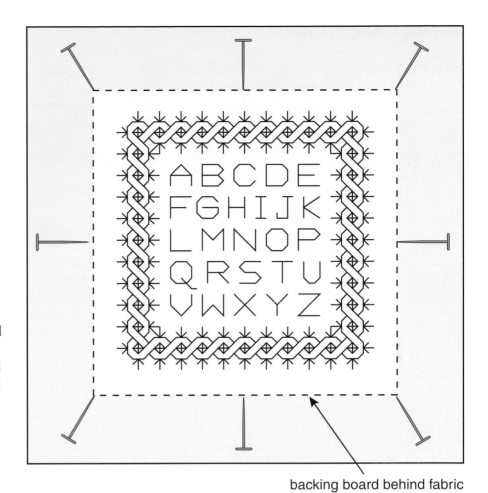

backing board behind fabric

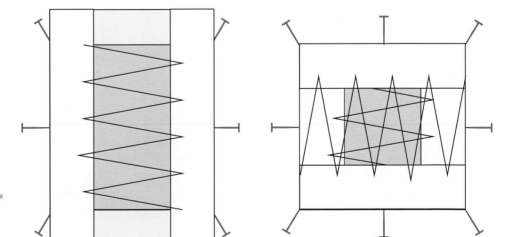

Making Custom Cording

Making your own cording is really easy and requires no special equipment. All you need are threads to match your project, a pencil, and your own two hands.

1. To make a length of cording, determine the amount you need and add ¼ more. For example, if you need 20 inches of finished cording, your measurement is 25 inches. Now double the amount for the cutting measurement: In this case it is now 50 inches.

2. Cut 2 or more lengths of matching floss or pearl cotton to the length of the cutting measurement. You can use all one color or multiple colors. Tie one end of the group of threads to a doorknob, and the other end to a pencil.

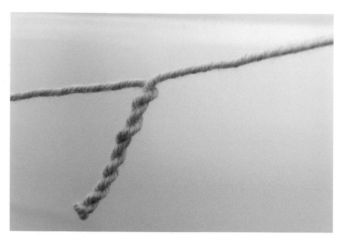

3. Next, twist the pencil, keeping the thread taut, until it starts to wind back onto itself when the tension is released slightly. This part of the process can take a while. Be careful not to drop your pencil or let the twist unwind or you'll have to start again.

4. When the thread has been wound with a sufficient amount of twist, fold the twisted length of thread in half and knot the end with the two groups of raw threads together as one. Your cording is now ready to use.

Attaching Cording to a Project

When attaching cording to a project, whether it is custom made to match your piece or prepurchased, you want the stitching to show as little as possible. It can be attached using a whip stitch using thread to match, if the cording is a solid color. When the cording is multicolored, use a neutral thread and work the whip stitch through the center of the cording rather than over the top of it, and your stitches will be nearly invisible.

Color Conversion and Metric Equivalent Charts

Color Conversion Chart

DMC thread numbers and names have been used in the projects in this book. If these threads are not available in your area, use the chart below to select the same colors for other brands of thread.

Color Name	DMC	Anchor	Sullivans	Color Name	DMC	Anchor	Sullivans
Dark lavender	209	109	45041	Dark topaz	782	307	45200
Medium red	304	1006	45050	Very dark cornflower blue	791	178	45202
Black	310	403	45053	Medium delft blue	799	136	45209
Dark violet	327	100	45065	Garnet	816	1005	45218
Navy	336	150	45069	Very dark coral red	817	13	45219
Dark coral	349	13	45073	Ultra dark beaver gray	844	1041	45241
Light coral	352	9	45076	Medium rose	899	52	45250
Very light pistachio green	369	1043	45082	Light parrot green	907	255	45256
Tan	436	1045	45097	Copper	921	1003	45267
Avocado green	469	267	45104	Light copper	922	1003*	45268
Light avocado green	470	267*	45105	Bright canary	973	297	45303
Very light avocado green	471	266	45106	Very dark forest green	986	246	45307
Light wedgewood	518	1039	45115	Forest green	989	242	45310
Violet	553	98	45125	Dark hunter green	3345	268	45342
Light violet	554	96	45126	Baby blue	3755	140	45378
Light cranberry	604	55	45139	Light peacock blue	3766	167	45383
Light old gold	676	891	45156	Very dark melon	3801	1098	45398
Medium light topaz	725	305	45170	Light celadon green	3817	875	45414
Medium old gold	729	890	45173	Dark straw	3820	306	45417
Light tangerine	742	303	45182	Medium bright turquoise	3845	1089	45443
Medium yellow	743	302	45184	Snow white	B5200	1	45002
Pale yellow	744	301	45185	White	blanc	2	45001

*No actual match. Closest match provided

Metric Equivalent Chart

1 inch = .254 centimeters
1 foot = 12 inches, 30.48 centimeters, or .30 meters
1 yard = 36 inches, 91.44 centimeters, or .91 meters

Glossary

Aida. A fabric used for cross-stitch that has an open weave with a mesh of squares. A single cross stitch is worked over each mesh square.

Appliqué. A decorative item cut from fabric and applied to the surface of another fabric.

Awl. A sharp tool used to punch through the fabric when making eyelets.

Counted thread. The process of working a stitch over a designated number of warp and weft threads in the fabric, usually following a charted pattern. The pattern is not premarked on the surface.

Crocking. Dye transference resulting from washing or handling an embroidered piece.

Edge finishing. Securing the raw edges of fabric to avoid fraying as you work. Can include hemming, or overstitching with either a zigzag sewing machine or a serger.

Embroidery. Decorative stitching in thread, floss, or yarn on a fabric ground.

Evenweave. Fabric with an identical number of warp and weft threads per inch. The individual threads in the fabric are easy to count and are used in counted-thread embroidery.

Floss. A common embroidery yarn, featuring six individual strands of thread that are separated before using.

Hank. Embroidery thread in a twisted, folded bundle. A hank must be prepared for use by trimming the double ends.

Laying tool. A sharp tool tapered at one end, used to flatten and guide threads into position. Using a laying tool helps ensure neat and tidy satin stitching.

Mercerization. A factory treatment for cotton threads that makes the thread stronger and adds a lustrous, shiny finish.

Pearl cotton. An embroidery yarn with 2-ply thread with an S-twist. The plies can't be separated. The finish features a high sheen and the yarn is sold in five sizes or weights: 3, 5, 8, 12, and 16. Sizez 5 and 8 are the most common.

Plainweave. Fabric with an identical number of warp and weft threads per inch. The individual threads in the fabric are tightly woven and difficult to count, making this a good fabric for surface embroidery projects.

Selvage. The tightly woven "self edge" on a woven fabric, created when the fabric is woven at the factory. This area of the fabric is unusable and should be trimmed away before cutting fabric for a project.

Skein. Embroidery thread in an easy-to-use bundle. The bundle is arranged so that the thread can be pulled from the skein to any desired length.

Straight pins. Pins of any length that have a small bead or ball at one end and a sharp point at the other. These are using to hold fabric sections together while sewing.

T-Pins. Larger pins with a sharp point at one end and a folded, T-shaped end at the other. These pins are easy to grab and hold, and are used to anchor fabric to completed projects to backings or blocking boards.

Thread count. The number of warp and weft threads per square inch of fabric. The higher the number, the tighter the weave.

Warp. Lengthwise threads in a plainweave or evenweave fabric.

Water-soluble. A product that can be dissolved in water.

Weft. Crosswise threads in a plainweave or evenweave fabric.

Sources

Online Retailers

If you don't have a needlework retailer in your area, or they don't stock the needed items, here are several suggestions for online retailers. This list is by no means complete, but they are companies that I have used and trust. A quick search using the keywords "embroidery materials and supplies" will yield an almost endless supply of options as well.

ABC Stitch
www.abcstitch.com

DMC USA Shopping
www.shopdmc.com

Herrschner's
www.herrschners.com

Nordic Needle
www.nordicneedle.com

Yarn Tree
http://yarntree.com/index.htm

Internet Inspiration

The internet is a terrific resource for learning more about embroidery, seeing what others are working on, and finding free patterns. Here are some of my favorite sites:

NeedleKnowledge
http://needleknowledge.com

About.com Embroidery
http://embroidery.about.com

About.com Cross Stitch
http://crossstitch.about.com

About.com Needlepoint
http://needlepoint.about.com

The Caron Collection
http://caron-net.com

Coats & Clark
http://coatsandclark.com

DMC's Emma's Broidery Blog
http://dmc-threads.com

DMC USA
http://dmc-usa.com

Kreinik
http://kreinik.com

Rainbow Gallery
http://rainbowgallery.com

ThreadWorx
http://threadworx.com

Index of Stitches

Algerian eyelet, 38
Back stitch, 20
Blanket stitch, 25
Buttonhole stitch, 26
Chain stitch, 22
Chain stitch pendant, 25
Chevron stitch, 28
Closed buttonhole stitch, 26
Closed herringbone stitch, 29
Colonial knot, 38
Coral stitch, 27
Couching, 45
Cross stitch, 40
Detached chain stitch, 23
Double chain stitch, 24
Double chevron stitch, 28
Double cross stitch/cross stitch star, 42
Double herringbone stitch, 29
Double running stitch, 18
Double seed stitch, 35
Ermine stitch, 36
Feather stitch, 31
Fern stitch, 31
Fishbone stitch, 33
Fly stitch, 32
Four-sided stitch, 43
French knot, 37
French knot with tail, 37
Hem stitch, 44
Herringbone stitch, 29
Holbein stitch, 43
Invisible stitch, 46

Knotted border stitch, 45
Laced running stitch, 19
Ladder stitch, 44
Lazy Daisy stitch, 23
Leaf stitch, 32
Long arm cross stitch, 41
Open Cretan stitch, 30
Padded satin stitch, 40
Running stitch, 17
Satin stitch flat, 39
Satin stitch outlined, 39
Scroll stitch, 28
Seed stitch, 35
Serpentine stitch, 44
Shisha mirror, attaching, 46
Split stitch, 21
Square chain stitch, 22
Stem stitch, 21
Straight stitch, 19
Threaded back stitch, 20
Tied herringbone stitch, 30
Tulip stitch, 36
Twisted border stitch, 45
Twisted chain stitch, 24
Up and down buttonhole stitch, 27
Upright cross stitch, 41
Van Dyke stitch, 33
Wheatear stitch, 34
Wheatear stitch detached, 34
Whip stitch, 46
Whipped running stitch, 18
Zigzag stitch, 42